THE BBC TV SHAKESPEARE

ALL'S WELL THAT ENDS WELL
ANTONY AND CLEOPATRA
AS YOU LIKE IT
HAMLET
HENRY IV Part 1
HENRY IV Part 2
HENRY V
HENRY VIII
JULIUS CAESAR
MEASURE FOR MEASURE
THE MERCHANT OF VENICE
RICHARD II
ROMEO AND JULIET
THE TAMING OF THE SHREW
THE TEMPEST
TWELFTH NIGHT
THE WINTER'S TALE

THE BBC TV SHAKESPEARE

Literary Consultant: John Wilders
Fellow of Worcester College, Oxford

The Taming of the Shrew

BRITISH BROADCASTING CORPORATION

Published by the
British Broadcasting Corporation
35 Marylebone High Street
London W1M 4AA

ISBN 0 563 17873 6

This edition first published 1980
© The British Broadcasting Corporation
and The Contributors 1980

The text of the Works of Shakespeare
edited by Peter Alexander
© William Collins Sons and Company Ltd 1951

The text of *The Taming of the Shrew* used in this volume is the Alexander
text, edited by the late Professor Alexander and chosen by the BBC as the
basis for its television production, and is reprinted by arrangement with
William Collins Sons and Company Ltd. The complete Alexander text is
published in one volume by William Collins Sons and Company Ltd under
the title *The Alexander Text of the Complete Works of William Shakespeare*.

All photographs are BBC copyright (David Green)

Printed in England at
The Pitman Press, Bath

CONTENTS

PREFACE

John Wilders

The Taming of the Shrew was printed in the first collected edition of Shakespeare's plays, the First Folio, published in 1623. It was probably written in 1593. An anonymous play, *The Taming of a Shrew*, which has many resemblances to Shakespeare's comedy, had, however, already appeared in print in 1594 and was for a long time thought to be the source of Shakespeare's comedy. It may possibly be itself an adaptation of a yet earlier play, now lost, from which both *A Shrew* and *The Shrew* were derived. The other sources of the plots of this play are discussed in the Introduction.

The first recorded production was given by the theatrical company for which Shakespeare consistently wrote, The Lord Chamberlain's Servants, in 1594 and it has been popular with theatre audiences ever since. Several adaptations were made and performed during the eighteenth century, usually by eliminating one or even two of the three plots and amplifying what was left. It was played in its entirety, possibly for the first time since the civil war period, in 1844 and with a minimum of scenery. Among the most successful interpreters of Katherina and Petruchio have been Edith Evans and Balliol Holloway, Sybil Thorndike and Lewis Casson, Diana Wynyard and Anthony Quayle, and Peggy Ashcroft and Peter O'Toole. A film version with Elizabeth Taylor and Richard Burton was directed by Franco Zeffirelli. This television production, directed by Jonathan Miller, was recorded at the BBC Television Centre in June 1980.

INTRODUCTION TO
THE TAMING OF THE SHREW

John Wilders

It was only very rarely that Shakespeare invented the plots of his plays. He usually took them from existing novels, plays or history books and adapted them freely for the stage. If we compare the plays with the works from which he adapted them, it becomes plain that, in shaping them for the theatre, he made them more exciting dramatically and more convincingly human. The account of the downfall and death of Richard II, for example, as told by the historian Holinshed, is flat and shapeless in comparison with Shakespeare's treatment of Holinshed's material. The historian conveys almost nothing of the King's psychological torment which, in Shakespeare's version, becomes the centre of our attention. The dramatist is able to place himself imaginatively in the position of the suffering monarch and to express the emotions of defiance, bewilderment, grief and betrayal which Richard would be likely to feel in his situation.

Shakespeare carried out a similar process of dramatic and psychological transformation as he developed the materials he drew on for his comedies, including *The Taming of the Shrew*, a very early play, written in about 1593, shortly after *Titus Andronicus* and before *The Two Gentlemen of Verona*. For this comedy he combined three different plots, each one taken from a different source. The story of the poor tinker who is deceived into believing he is a noble lord (which forms the Prologue to the play and is omitted from this production as being unsuitable for the medium of television) belongs to folklore; the story of the rebellious daughter who is tamed into a submissive wife had already been the subject of many tales and ballads; and the story of the nobleman who changes roles with his servant and gains access to the woman he loves was taken from an existing play, *The Supposes* by George Gascoigne, itself a translation from an Italian comedy, *I Suppositi*, by the poet Ariosto. By combining and interweaving the three stories Shakespeare created a number of striking contrasts: between the apparently meek but actually wilful Bianca and the boldly rebellious but finally submissive Katherina; between Lucentio's romantic infatuation with Bianca and Petruchio's unashamedly mercenary marriage to her sister; between the secretive, devious courtship of the younger sister by her suitors and the resolutely open seizure of Katherina by Petruchio. Moreover, as Christopher Sly is persuaded that he is 'a lord indeed' because he is treated as though he were one, so Kate is gradually induced to become 'pleasant, gamesome, passing courteous' because her husband repeatedly assures her, in the face of the evidence, that she is so. Shakespeare thus gives to the central characters and situations a strength and vividness absent from the original versions by inviting us to compare and contrast them with one another, and, at the lowest level, the mixture of plots offers the audience the pleasure of variety.

In writing *The Taming of the Shrew*, however, he did a great deal more than cunningly interweaving three hitherto separate stories. One of his most substantial additions was to place them in a solidly recognisable social context. Like nearly all his comedies, this is a family play dealing with the domestic processes of courtship and marriage, and its action (like that of *Much Ado About Nothing* and *Twelfth Night*) is placed appropriately in a domestic establishment – or, rather, two of them: the house of the father, Baptista, in which the marriages are arranged, and that of the husband, Petruchio, to which the couple move after their marriage.

Baptista belongs to a social class which had become prominent by the end of the sixteenth century. Successful, prosperous city merchants of his kind had been increasing in number and power as a result of the development of London as a port, as a centre of the manufacturing industries, and as a base for the imports of silks, spices and precious metals from the Indies and the export of cloth to Europe. Some Elizabethan merchants were richer than the old aristocracy, and the latter were not uncommonly in debt to them or attempted to preserve their dwindling fortunes by selling to them the estates which their families had owned through generations. Although Baptista has an Italian name and lives in Padua, his type would be immediately recognisable to an English audience.

He is identified quite early in the play as 'very rich', not a member of the aristocracy but 'an affable and courteous gentleman'. Like many fathers of his class, he is anxious that his children should make financially sound and socially acceptable **marriages**. Hence he needs to be assured that their suitors are well off and come from families similar to his own. This is the reason for the repeated interest by the characters of this play in names and parentage. Lucentio declares himself to be the son of 'Vincentio, come of the Bentivolii', 'a merchant of great traffic through the world'. Petruchio, introducing himself to his prospective father-in-law, identifies himself as 'Antonio's son, A man well known throughout all Italy', and the sole heir to his father's estate. Again, the disguised Tranio assumes that he will not be allowed to woo Bianca until he has supplied her father with 'knowledge of his parentage'. It is within this socially and financially exclusive world that Tranio is comically exposed as 'the son of a sailmaker in Bergamo'.

The rich fathers who appear in the background of this play take care to educate their children in a manner appropriate to their station in life. Lucentio arrives in Padua (an ancient and distinguished university town in Shakespeare's time) in order to educate himself in rhetoric, logic and the ethical works of Aristotle, the foundation of the renaissance university curriculum, and Baptista gladly admits to his house the tutors who will instruct his daughters in the arts of music and Latin poetry. It is by means of such realistic details that Shakespeare gives life and body to a series of conventional – indeed improbable – situations.

He also creates domestic biographies for Bianca's suitors. Old Gremio speaks of his 'house within the city', which suggests that he, too, is a merchant, and, indeed, he is called Baptista's 'neighbour'. This splendid mansion

> Is richly furnished with plate and gold,
> Basins and ewers to lave her dainty hands;
> My hangings all of Tyrian tapestry;
> In ivory coffers I have stuff'd my crowns;
> In Cypress chests my arras counterpoints,
> Costly apparel, tents, and canopies,
> Fine linen, Turkey cushions boss'd with pearl,
> Valance of Venice gold in needle-work;
> Pewter and brass, and all things that belongs
> To house or housekeeping.

In strong contrast, Christopher Sly, the itinerant tinker of the Prologue, for all his boasts to be descended from the supporters of 'Richard Conqueror', has apparently no home and no clothing other than the doublet, stockings and worn-out shoes he stands up in.

Whereas Gremio's is a city establishment within the walls of Padua, Petruchio's is apparently a country estate which has to be reached on horseback along muddy roads. Shakespeare creates an even more lifelike and convincing impression of his house but by different means, through the conversation between his servants shortly before the master's homecoming with his bride. The dramatist knows intimately the wisecracking comradeship which exists among servants, their curiosity about their new mistress, and their eagerness to provide her with a decent, formal welcome. In the instructions of the chief servant, Grumio, to his inferiors, Shakespeare offers us a sudden glimpse into an Elizabethan household and the relationships between its members:

> Where's the cook? Is supper ready, the house trimm'd, rushes strew'd, cobwebs swept, the serving-men in their new fustian, their white stockings, and every officer his wedding garment on? Be the jacks fair within, the jills fair without, the carpets laid, and everything in order? . . . Call forth Nathaniel, Joseph, Nicholas, Philip, Walter, Sugarsop, and the rest; let their heads be sleekly comb'd, their blue coats brush'd and their garters of an indifferent knit; let them curtsy with their left legs, and not presume to touch a hair of my master's horse-tail till they kiss their hands. Are they all ready?

As well as sketching in the physical details of the house, Shakespeare suggests that Petruchio commands a well-disciplined establishment, and should therefore have no trouble in controlling his wife.

The action of *The Taming of the Shrew* is therefore set in a carefully documented social context, that of the Elizabethan mercantile upper-middle class. Its senior member, Baptista, sets about finding husbands for his daughters in the customary manner of his class and time. It was the usual practice of aristocratic or rich parents to arrange their children's marriages for them and, in so doing, they considered money was as important – usually more important – than any feelings the young couple might have for each other. Indeed, the prospective bride and groom sometimes did not meet until the financial arrangements had been made between the parents and formally set down in a legal contract. By more or less auctioning off his younger daughter to the highest bidder (Act II Scene i), Baptista is behaving no more callously towards her than would any father of his time and rank. On the contrary, like Juliet's father when he arranges her marriage to the County Paris, he displays what Shakespeare's contemporaries would have seen as a proper concern for his daughter's welfare, a desire for her to live in the state to which she has been accustomed. In fact, by insisting that Katherina's husband should first obtain 'that special thing . . . her love', he shows more consideration for her feelings than would the average Elizabethan parent. The bad marriage in this play is made by Lucentio who, romantically infatuated with Bianca, fails to realise that beneath her show of meekness she is a wilfully independent girl.

Petruchio, since his father is dead, has the freedom to arrange his own marriage, and he too sets about it in the manner of his time. Initially he wants to marry in order to enrich his estate and, on hearing that a wealthy bride is available, introduces himself to her father, shows that he comes from a respectable family, assures him that his finances are in good shape, accepts his offer of a dowry, and proposes that the contract should be drawn up forthwith:

Let specialities be therefore drawn between us,
That covenants may be kept on either hand.

It is only then that he asks to meet for the first time the woman he has already agreed to marry. Petruchio is unorthodox not in procedure but in the rapidity and singlemindedness with which he carries it out.

Shakespeare goes to considerable trouble, therefore, to create for this play a solid, vivid, detailed and consistent social setting and to make the minor characters behave according to the orthodoxies of their class. This is an impressive achievement in itself, but when we look at the unorthodox characters, Petruchio and Katherina, in the setting Shakespeare has provided for them, we can see how necessary that environment is for the play's comic and psychological effects.

Why Katherina is a shrew we are not told, but her shrewishness consists of rebelling violently against the conventions by which the rest of the household lives. She challenges the authority of her father, secretly torments her younger sister (in what may be thought of as a jealous fit in the nursery), breaks a lute over her music tutor's head, and reviles her prospective husband at first sight. The impropriety of her conduct is the more startling, and the funnier, because of the obvious propriety of the rest of the family and the consequent social embarrassment they undergo. Moreover, we can understand her defiance of the rules as an assertion of her independence, an unwillingness to conform to the code of bourgeois materialism and respectability observed by the other characters, and a refusal to be sold in the marriage market as though she had no character of her own. As a result she has too much character. In rebelling against her background she shows herself, in her own way, to be as much a product of it as the apparently conventional Bianca.

She presents to Petruchio two connected problems. In order to transform her from a virago into a tolerable wife, he has to induce in her a respect for and obedience to the social conventions she has hitherto been accustomed to defy, and he must also win from her 'that special thing . . . her love' on which her father had insisted. He solves the first problem by flouting social decorum even more violently than his wife. On the day of his marriage he keeps her waiting outside the church, arrives for the ceremony dressed like a ragamuffin, swears in front of the parson, and,

> after many ceremonies done
> He calls for wine: 'A health!' quoth he, as if
> He had been aboard, carousing to his mates
> After a storm; quaff'd off the muscadel,
> And threw the sops all in the sexton's face . . .
> This done, he took the bride about the neck,
> And kiss'd her lips with such a clamorous smack
> That at the parting all the church did echo.

Finally, as the guests assemble for the customary wedding feast, he carries the bride off and leaves them, astonished, to go in without the two principal guests. The immediate effect of his behaviour is to create acute social embarrassment, not only for Baptista who is worried about his reputation with his neighbours ('What will be said? What mockery will it be?') but for Katherina herself who bursts into tears. Petruchio is, as they say, 'more shrew than she', and by depriving his wife of the usual formalities of marriage, arouses in her a desire for those very social proprieties she has hitherto defied. He begins to make her realise that the rituals that society observes – the wedding garments, the solemn liturgy, the gathering of friends and neighbours – are not necessarily meaningless conventions or displays of wealth, but forms through which the significance of marriage is expressed. He sees directly through the outward forms to the truths they are designed to reveal. For example, when Baptista begs him to dress more suitably, his retort is,

To me she's married, not unto my clothes.

So far Petruchio has merely denied his wife the customs proper to marriage. Once he has snatched her from her family, however, his treatement becomes more radical: he deprives her of the sheer necessities – food, clothing and sleep – on which domestic life must be based. *The Taming of the Shrew* is a play which in performance requires a great many solid household objects – boots, a basin of water, dishes of food, a hat and a lady's gown. In themselves they are not important but, for Katherina, they are made to become important because she needs them, and her husband not only denies her the use of them but flings them away. His treatment of them comes to seem like a kind of sacrilege. The woman who had shown her hostility to convention, and had broken that domestic object a lute over her teacher's head, now comes to recognise their real value. By undergoing a course of social education in Petruchio's 'taming school' she learns the value of good housekeeping.

Petruchio solves his other problem, the winning of her love, by treating her throughout her ordeal as though she were lovable:

Say that she rail; why, then I'll tell her plain
She sings as sweetly as a nightingale.
Say that she frown; I'll say she looks as clear
As morning roses newly wash'd with dew.
Say she be mute, and will not speak a word;
Then I'll commend her volubility,
And say she uttereth piercing eloquence.

He starves her of food and sleep while assuring her that it is done 'in reverend care of her' and, as a result, she is not so much browbeaten forcibly into submission (and it was not uncommon for women of Katherina's temperament to be thrashed by their husbands) as induced psychologically to respect and need him. She comes to depend on him partly for the images of herself he reflects back at her. 'The mind sees not itself,' says Brutus in *Julius Caesar*, 'But by reflection, by some other things.' The reflection of herself which Katherina sees in Petruchio is a very attractive one. Of course she also finds herself dependent on him for her material needs and learns that, if she is to lead a tolerable life, she must subordinate her will to his. This is a belief with which few twentieth-century audiences would agree and, for this reason, *The Taming of the Shrew* may well appear a repellently chauvinistic play. But it was a belief held by the vast majority of Shakespeare's own audience, especially those of the bourgeois, merchant class in the portrayal of which he took such care. He includes in the play their assumptions as well as their way of life. How far he himself agreed with them we cannot know; as always, he remains true to his characters, which is not necessarily the same as being true to his own beliefs. It is more than likely that he agreed with them.

The comedy ends with an injunction by Katherina to all wives to obey their husbands, and her words recall those of St Paul's Epistle to the Ephesians:

> Wives, submit yourselves unto your own husbands, as unto the Lord. For the husband is the head of the wife, even as Christ is the head of the church: and he is the saviour of the body. Therefore as the church is subject unto Christ, so let the wives be to their own husbands in every thing.

Her concluding homily is at the same time a celebration of the domestic security of the family which she sees as dependent on the subordination of wife to husband:

> Thy husband is thy lord, thy life, thy keeper,
> Thy head, thy sovereign; one that cares for thee,
> And for thy maintenance commits his body
> To painful labour both by sea and land,
> To watch the night in storms, the day in cold,
> Whilst thou liest warm at home, secure and safe.

Even in the composition of this closing speech Shakespeare remained true to the attitudes of his age, for there was, in the England of his time, an increasing respect for the institution of marriage, partly under the influence of Puritanism. As Lawrence Stone has pointed out in *The Family, Sex and Marriage in England 1500–1800* (a book on which much of this Introduction is based), 'the sanctification of marriage – "holy matrimony" – was a constant theme of Protestant sermons of the sixteenth century, which were directed to all classes in society, and is to be found in both Puritan and Anglican theology of the early seventeenth century'. He also notes that a new motive for marriage was introduced into the Prayer Book of 1549. It was defended not only for 'the avoidance of fornication, and the procreation of legitimate children', but for the 'mutual society, help and comfort that the one ought to have of the other, both in prosperity and in adversity'. It was in order to underline the play's religious as well as social defence of matrimony that Jonathan Miller, the director of this television production, decided to conclude it with the singing of a Puritan hymn, a paraphrase of one of the psalms, in which marriage is celebrated not as a social convention but as a manifestation of the ideal relationship between man, woman and God. We shall misunderstand this play if we assume that Shakespeare is always, as he was called not long ago, 'our contemporary'.

THE PRODUCTION

Henry Fenwick

At the first read-through of *The Taming of the Shrew* Jonathan Miller, who is directing as well as producing, explains his overall approach to the play to the assembled actors. It is a very serious approach: 'One should creep up in camouflage,' he declares, 'and find out it's funny later on.' It's not to be approached looking for the laughs. Any past productions they may have seen which trade in a sort of 'romping, tumbling merriment', must be forgotten. All that is to be avoided. 'Oh?' says John Cleese, the rather unconventionally cast Petruchio, 'shall I leave now?'

He is, however, being disingenuous. Any preconception, drawn from his manically inspired comic work in *Monty Python* or *Fawlty Towers*, that he is a knockabout clown is totally wrong. He's a very serious, careful, hard-thinking man and it was the seriousness of Miller's approach which attracted him in the first place. 'I called Jonathan,' he explains, 'to ask a question about something completely separate and he called me back five minutes later and said, "What do you think of Shakespeare?" And I said "I find it extremely difficult to enjoy." He said, "Would you look at *The Taming of the Shrew*?" and I said yes. I also said, "I'm very dubious because I have a vague memory of the play; but I'll certainly read it and then let's talk about it." My reaction at that stage was very sceptical because I had a vague memory of *The Shrew* as being about a lot of furniture getting knocked over and a lot of wine being spilled and a lot of thighs being slapped and a lot of unmotivated laughter – and also what Jonathan later dubbed "twinkling". The actors stand there with their heads bobbing ever so slightly from side to side, twinkling at each other.

'I also had a considerable problem with Shakespeare, which is that I don't like the way 98% of it is acted: no, that's a little unfair – 90%. I enjoyed Olivier's *Richard III* because I thought that was terrific fun, and I thought Jonathan Pryce's *Hamlet* recently was super, but on the whole it seems to lend itself to declamation and that seems to me to be death: at that point I'd rather read it. Also I think he's fairly bad on plots, which nobody seems to own up to – though they do if you talk to them for a long time. And there is a general reverence about Shakespeare which I always think is a deathly quality, whatever you're talking about. When I read the play I wasn't enormously impressed, but I began to get interested, and Jonathan then came and I asked him what I thought were some very tough, specific questions about how one would make that point work, how do you do this speech without creating such and such an effect, and he gave me such good answers that I became convinced that you could make it work, that an actor could make it work.'

'Although it's a play with a great deal of fun in it,' says Miller, 'the fun must arise out of a very concrete, realistic situation, not out of a determination to have a romp! I approached the play very much in the light of certain assumptions about families, ancient and modern, about fathers and their daughters, and also about the peculiar character of sixteenth-century families in which the authority of the father and husband is a *sine qua non* of the family being smoothly run. You can't slip and slide around that notion of obedience just because it offends our beliefs about the independence of women: they did not think that way then and there is no way in which you can actually equivocate about it. You've simply got to say well, whether we like it or not, that's what they thought. It may not coincide with what we think, but what we think is really quite beside the point. If everything is done in the light of what we think it's a sort of historical egocentricity which is quite intolerable, I think; what T. S. Eliot calls "historical provincialism".'

The only cut Miller took was to remove the Induction – that odd and unresolved framework of the beggar Sly being duped and entertained by a wealthy lord. Its removal is by no means new, and not only did it tidy the play considerably, it also helped the seriousness of the approach. 'You can come on straight,' Miller explains. 'I was interested in certain aspects of Elizabethan puritanism – the Puritan squirearchy and the idea of the moral seriousness of Petruchio rather than his cavalierish twinkle, which is the usual way it is done. There's a certain sort of moral gravity, which I think actually is there in Cleese: underneath the fun and humour of the man there is an intensity.'

Miller's ideas were shaped, he says, by reading Laurence Stone's *Marriage, Sex and the Family* and also a book by Michael Walzer called *The Revolution of the Saints*, 'a book on the rise of the Elizabethan puritan movement and the bringing back of the

Calvinist notions of a fallen world, one which required magistrates and disciplinarians to keep order in a fallen, naughty world which has inherited congenitally the sin of Adam. Cleese lent himself to that conception and asked to be given ideas which would embody that central notion. And naturally he brought to it that peculiar, unparaphrasable quality which is him, which was the dense centre of the work. But around him were a lot of extremely competitive and capable actors who gave him a good run for his money. There was very vigorous and forceful competition from Sarah [Badel – Kate] and Anthony Pedley [Tranio] – from all of them. The thing that was nice about John was that a lot of stars are made anxious by other people getting laughs. He was always delighted by the laughs other people got.'

In keeping with the seriousness of the approach, the sets are pared back, but far from simple in conception. Colin Lowrey, who designed the *Antony and Cleopatra* for Jonathan, showed me the wide range of his source material. The base is a mid-sixteenth-century stage-setting by Serlio with doorways and loggias and alleys, but it has gone through several influences on its way to Television Centre Studio One. He has used Dutch paintings to give him ideas for the interiors, for texture, for lighting; further ideas for texture and lighting come from the pictures of Edward Hopper; but most important of all is the influence of de Chirico – the basic Italian sixteenth-century conception has gone through a twentieth-century rethinking and transformation. The Renaissance arches, the multiplicity of doors and corridors, have suffered a change into a more streamlined modern consciousness. And perhaps most important of all was the final overriding simplicity: 'We were looking at the model and Jonathan said, "Isn't it a pity that we can't make that model twenty feet high, no paint, nothing," and we thought, Well, why can't we. So we stripped everything back to the bare plywood.' The effect is to emphasise the shapes, the structure of the set, and also to give a Puritan austerity. 'It was very difficult to achieve,' says Lowrey. He points to a Vermeer reproduction: 'If you take as a starting point two things – first the directional light coming through the windows, and second the surface texture – that is the basis of the set; but out of that you've got to subtract all the Dutch detailing – all the dark, framed paintings – and somehow add the Italian into that. You keep that Dutch floor, that directional lighting, that texture of the wall, a series of rooms like that, but all the detailing is taken out, then we've "de Chiricoed" it – it's a matter of learning to think like de Chirico: copying the details and then abstracting it.'

The costumes, too, are beautiful and subdued. Alun Hughes has gone to de la Tour and Caravaggio for his references. 'The first thing was to look out for the colour – we kept a low profile on the painter's palette. Jonathan wanted things very simple, not a lot of decoration. The action was taking place in late summer, early September time of year, so it wasn't too formal and we kept to ambers and earth colours. For Lucentio, for example, I used Manfredi's *The Lute Player* but I toned down the red of the costume to a burnt orange. Kate and Bianca I had in similar colour ranges but I started Bianca in lighter colours, gradually darkening, and Kate started darker and lightens. And the interest comes from contrasting texture.' The most difficult part was finding materials which would have the faded, broken-down qualities wanted. Hughes went round buying up a lot of curtains which had faded in the sun: 'It gives more depth to the folds without using too much fabric,' he explains, 'and the colour changes are like painter's highlights. It saves breaking down new material – and it saves money!'

When Miller was working on *Antony and Cleopatra* he had told me that when he approached a play he didn't approach it with any clear idea of what to do – it formed itself in rehearsal. Yet his ideas about the *Shrew* seem very firm. I ask him about this apparent contradiction. 'I usually have a *general* idea, then let it shape up as I find the people,' he explains. 'The people have a very strong material influence on what the play is going to be. Whatever ideas you have about them are very often altered by the actual substance that is going to embody them, and there is no way you can impose an idea on an actor who is going to play it. Obviously one has to give them a general idea to which they must consent in order to work, but the moment to moment details of a production are very very much determined by what they bring to it. And if you've got really good and talented actors they always bring an unprecedented thing. And quite apart from the fact that each person brings an idiosyncracy which you can't forecast, there is also no way in which merely by reading the play over and over to yourself you can ever become acquainted with what's being said in that play. The phrase I always go back to is a phrase of Peter Strausen, Professor of Philosophy at Oxford: he said it was a mistake to believe that sentences mean things, although in a very general linguistic sense they mean things; but the full meaning of a sentence cannot be got till you've understood that *sentences* don't mean things so much as *people* mean things by the sentences they utter. It's always said by literary critics that you ought to be able to know what a character is from the sum of all that is actually said in a play by that given character; but if that were the case, then every time the play is performed the character would be the same. What is so peculiar about a play is that every time it's performed by a different actor, under the guidance of a different director, you're actually meeting someone quite new. As director, in order to find what is meant by a particular sentence, you and the actor have to improvise what that particular person means by the sentence they're using. And you can't do that until you've somehow improvised a biography for them; in the end you have to invent a person not entirely made up of all the things they say in the play.'

If that sounds complex, it's a complexity the actors are very happy to live with. 'With Jonathan everybody is important,' says Susan Penhaligon, who plays Bianca. 'I know every director will *say* that but when it comes down to rehearsing, because of time or whatever, a lot of directors don't put it into practice. Jonathan does. He creates an atmosphere where you can go up to him at any time and talk for half an hour about your character – even if you've got two lines he'll build up a whole background for you so you know what you're saying.

'I wanted to make as much as I could of Bianca and I realised that she is as strong as Kate but had probably dealt with the family situation better than Kate; she'd learned to get her own way by smiling, by being a bit sweeter, but in the fight scene she fights just as hard! They both want to get away from this very tedious life, trapped in the house, not being able to go out, and I think Bianca likes fun but she can't get out till her sister gets married. This is what causes the rows between her and Kate, all day long, and that's on top of the initial arguments that started probably when they were children because Bianca was spoiled. Bianca sees this goodlooking guy and decides that's what she wants, but once she's married to him she's going to be boss. *She* turns out to be the shrew and she'll treat him *very* badly. The lovely thing I think about the way Sarah has played it is that Kate has learned how to love, Kate has learned how to give, Petruchio has shown her: Bianca has got her own way all her life and goes on getting her own way. I certainly think in the end Bianca loses out! I know that I've got a man I can control. Shakespeare is saying something about women and love and marriage. I've always found that final speech of Kate's difficult to take: "Place your hands below your husband's foot"! I just loved the way Sarah did it, what she got out of it: unless you give you're not going to get anything out of a relationship. It isn't really about women's role in life, it's about – maybe – how you love!'

'We started with it as a story and almost forgot it was Shakespeare,' says Cleese. 'I was a bit worried about having to speak verse, and Jonathan said it was his experience that most people with my kind of voice – which is sort of your standard middle-class newsreader's voice, people who naturally pronounce consonants fairly clearly – didn't have too much trouble with it. Then, in order to ask him a question, I quoted something – a couple of lines I wanted to discuss – and before he answered the question he said, "Incidentally, I'd like you to speak the verse just as you read it then." And I suddenly thought, "Ah, I can do this, I'm not being asked to declaim or be a Shakespearian actor; I'm just being asked to say the words, as Jonathan later put it, to get the meaning out of it." If you say it to get the meaning across then all the business about the rhythm of the verse falls into place.

'The facinating thing I did learn – and it increased by respect for Shakespeare hugely – was that if there is a line in the text and you don't know how to say it, if you keep on thinking about it and leave your mind open you suddenly see how it should be said: there's a moment when you think: "That's what he meant, that's how you make it work." Very often watching Shakespeare it has nothing to do with people you and I know, it's as though the actors had recently arrived on a space craft from another planet and all they know about life on earth is from watching a series of tapes of other people playing Shakespeare. There is one point in the play when Petruchio goes into this very flowery language, very strange, and it became obvious to me that it had to be a send-up, so I said to Jonathan, "Can I do it like X?" – and I threw in three or four of the gestures which irritate me when I'm watching Shakespearian acting I don't like, and one or two of those meaningless hanging inflections. So there's a little bit of send-up of the sort of Shakespearian acting I don't like stuck in the middle of the play. I am sure when Shakespeare wrote that speech, had he not been able to go over to the actor and say, "Look, when you come to that speech, it's a send-up, OK?", if he hadn't been there to do that, then I'm sure he'd have put "archly" in brackets.'

Miller's emphasis on the Puritan background to the character proved, Cleese says, very useful: 'It didn't mean much to me at first but once he'd given me that thread I was able to use it to determine my attitude to other people. Like Tranio – I think Petruchio smells a rat there straightaway – he doesn't like people who pretend to be what they're not. Though he's a fairly wealthy guy, he would sit down with a carpenter – to borrow a phrase of Gurdjieff – anyone who made a good cup of coffee would be of interest to him, but he doesn't like poseurs. And we'd come across odd bits of the text and think, Oh yes, that fits! All the stuff about dress and clothes made a good deal of sense: he's saying outward appearances don't matter. He's not a monster – he makes sure the tailor gets paid – but he feels all this frippery is nonsense. And if anyone said, "How could you treat people like this, play such a terrible practical joke?", I'm sure he would say, "Do 'em good! Make 'em think!"

'I have a very dear friend, a psychiatrist, an older man than myself, and I got him to read the play. He said that when Kate and Petruchio meet for the first time he was laughing out loud because that is exactly what he does with shrews – that took my breath away; but he also said that this particular technique of sending them up only works if it is done with genuine love. If you send people up without that love and affection it doesn't work. They have to trust, they have to stay open. They change by the process of examining themselves, but if it isn't done with warmth then they will close off.

'One doesn't want to portray Petruchio as too awful, yet you could very easily. He says, "I come to wive it wealthily", he says it quite clearly and you can't talk your way out of it. He hears that Kate's a very rich girl and he makes up his mind to marry her. But two things emerged for me: the first is that something happens when he sees her for the first time; the second is that he obviously has an attitude – which may be more or less right – that women have a good deal in common, that he knows a good deal about women and he probably feels it doesn't greatly matter which woman you get because if you treat her in the right way she will become a good wife. Then when he sees Kate something over and above that happens.

'It's very intriguing to talk about these countries where there are still arranged marriages and a lot of them finish up as very happy marriages, whereas in our day, here, where everybody appears to be free to choose, a lot of marriages, a very high proportion, go wrong – and not just the ones that end up in divorce. It may be something to do with the acceptance of the other person and the relationship: how do I get the best out of it instead of how do I get out of it? If you actually say, "Right, I'm in this, now how do I actually make it work?" maybe the thing does start working.'

Playing the eventually tamed shrew, Sarah Badel had probably the most difficult task for a twentieth-century woman. 'I didn't lay anything down for myself,' she says. 'I just thought, "I'm going to throw myself into a black hole and do it!" I don't think Kate is living in her head at all; I don't think her behaviour is calculated. It's very difficult, actually, because I think that what people say about her you have to fulfil: you can't just suggest a frustrated bluestocking or an intelligent woman at odds with society or any other fashionable view of it. Her dialogue when one comes to think of it has nothing very profound or witty. She's hardly a dazzling intellect. Her language would have to be much cleverer if she were a woman who had reviewed her situation and could be in command of it: it hasn't the lyricism of Viola or the wit of Beatrice. There has to be something to drive her beyond what anyone can cope with. She's a woman of such passion, or that's how I saw it, a woman of such enormous capacity for love, that the only way she could be happy is to find a man of equal capacity. Therefore she's made for lack of love.

'It's interesting how often madness is mentioned – almost the first thing that's said about her is "That wench is stark mad"; and almost the first thing that's said about Petruchio is he's mad. He feigns madness; she in my view is teetering on the edge of it. Her behaviour is very provocative. Her father can't protect her because she will not be protected: she lays herself wide open to ridicule and abuse. I think she's living very dangerously behaving like this, but I don't believe it's calculated. I think it's a clarion call, a declaration of self: she can't find anyone, she can't do anything! I think she's a woman with no talent except one, which is her capacity to love a man to her utmost, but all the men are turning tail and running the other way! That's the comedy of it. If you simply have something shrewish it's rather tiresome and ugly and you feel "Oh, shut up!" It has to have tremendous range. She's a woman of passion and that's the comedy, that's the frustration, that's the tightrope she walks. She lays herself open to ridicule and I think she has to be ridiculous, otherwise the men in the play become very unpleasant, it makes their attitude to her insensitive. She has to go that far, she has to be extreme, to justify what's said about her. She is impossible. She's driving them all mad, I think.

'There's no point in thinking about it or defending yourself with intelligent approaches – you simply have to come on with a total declaration and not care what anybody thinks about you, because she doesn't. She's a father's nightmare, for any father who loves her, and I'm sure he does. It's easy to put the blame on the father: it's very much the fashion. I think people now find it a very difficult play and so they think, "Oh, it's her father's fault", but I think he's doing his damnedest in that society. What else could he do? In fact there's a very interesting speech, when she rounds on her father and says:

"She must have a husband;
I must dance bare-foot on her wedding-day,
And for your love to her lead apes in hell."

The only person who could speak that speech with justification is Bianca. It's quite mad! And he's using Bianca as bait – all these suitors coming to the house round the honeypot of Bianca, and he's just hoping that one will fly off and buzz his eldest!

'I think she's driven by fear – the overriding fear of being an old maid, of missing out on it all at the beginning. Then when she does meet a man who is for her there's the fear of the feelings he produces in her for the first time in her life. Something's got to give! It has been a reign of terror and in a way she has been enjoying it, though it comes from a very real distress. She can't see herself at all: all she can see is other people's reactions to her, running a mile appalled. Petruchio is the only man who shows her what she's like. He is the man who stands in front of her and she goes Whack! across the face and he says, OK, but if you do it again you'll get Whack! from me: She's at liberty to do it again – he can take anything she cares to dish out, and therefore she's safe for the first time in her life. He doesn't in the least enjoy the fisticuffs but in her screams and howls and exhibitions she's making of herself he does see what others don't and he has to get through all that because he loves her.'

As for the final speech, the one that nowadays people find so hard to accept? 'You mean the speech to make Germaine Greer sick?' she says. 'That's a love speech to him. For the first time she realises the extreme vulnerability of men. She was so vulnerable herself before that she couldn't see it at all! But on the road back to Padua, which is a crucial transition scene, he finally makes her laugh, she laughs at herself – a bit like *Ninotchka* – and she sees exactly what he's done for her. She's found release. That's how she finds her tongue at the end and can be eloquent.'

In fact, the final scene of the play, when I saw it, I found not only funny and satisfying but also unexpectedly moving. Miller has ended the play with the family around the table, singing a psalm. 'I did a production of *The Shrew* a long time ago at Chichester,' he explained to me, 'and there we used a rather serious hymn about marriage by Purcell. I wanted something comparable. The use of a psalm, the use of holy music as a celebratory theme, was very important to me. I felt it brought it together – in music is the spirit of reconciliation, but also the words of that particular psalm are to do with the fruitful vine of the family. It is the orderly, peaceful fruitfulness of the family which I think the play is about; it's about the attempt to restore order in a disorderly world, duty in a rebellious world.

' "At last, though long, our jarring notes agree" is what Lucentio says at the beginning of that last scene: all these jarring notes have been reconciled. As so often in Shakespeare music is used as a metaphor for the restoration of harmony, the restoration of social order. For the sixteenth century there are metaphysical mystical significances attached to music – the idea that there is in music some higher order, a Pythagorean order of numbers, of proportion and harmony to which human life aspires and only occasionally reaches. I think that in these plays there are moments of sublime pause and settlement when human beings in their mortal muddy state do nevertheless transcend themselves and reach states of harmony.' *The Shrew* is not a play people normally find such harmony in, but it looks very strongly as though Miller has succeeded.

THE BBC TV CAST AND
PRODUCTION TEAM

The cast for the BBC Television production was as follows:

PETRUCHIO	John Cleese
KATHERINA	Sarah Badel
LUCENTIO	Simon Chandler
TRANIO	Anthony Pedley
BAPTISTA	John Franklyn-Robbins
GREMIO	Frank Thornton
HORTENSIO	Jonathan Cecil
BIANCA	Susan Penhaligon
BIONDELLO	Harry Waters
GRUMIO	David Kincaid
VINCENTIO	John Barron
PEDANT	John Bird
WIDOW	Joan Hickson
CURTIS	Angus Lennie
BAPTISTA'S SERVANT	Bev Willis
NATHANIEL	Harry Webster
PHILIP	Gil Morris
GREGORY	Leslie Sarony
NICHOLAS	Derek Deadman
PETER	Denis Gilmore
TAILOR	Alan Hay
HABERDASHER	David Kinsey

PRODUCTION ASSISTANT	Alan Charlesworth
DIRECTOR'S ASSISTANT	Patricia Preece
PRODUCTION UNIT MANAGER	Fraser Lowden
MUSIC	Stephen Oliver
LITERARY CONSULTANT	John Wilders
MAKE-UP ARTIST	Eileen Mair
COSTUME DESIGNER	Alun Hughes
SOUND	Chick Anthony

LIGHTING	John Treays
DESIGNER	Colin Lowrey
SCRIPT EDITOR	David Snodin
PRODUCER	Jonathan Miller
DIRECTOR	Jonathan Miller

The production was recorded between 18 and 24 June 1980

THE TEXT

The Taming of the Shrew, based loosely on a play entitled 'The Taming of a Shrew' and also on a story by Ariosto (although Shakespeare must have encountered this story in an English adaptation of Ariosto's 'Suppositi' by George Gascoigne), was probably written about 1594. It was first published in the folio edition of Shakespeare's works printed in 1623, which contained the entire canon apart from *Pericles*. Further folios appeared in 1632, 1663, 1664 and 1685. The first critical edition of the works, edited by Nicholas Rowe, appeared in 1709. It is to Rowe that we owe many stage-directions, and the division of the plays into acts and scenes. Since then, innumerable editions have been published, with countless emendations and 'improvements'. The text printed here is that prepared by the late Professor Peter Alexander for his edition of the *Complete Works*, first published in 1951. This is the text used for all the productions in the BBC TV series.

Under Jonathan Miller's rule as producer of the series, we have at all times tried to remain aware of the fact that every play will be seen by millions of people who have never seen, or indeed read, a Shakespeare play before; and that these people should therefore be given the chance to see a version of the play that sticks as faithfully as possible to the text. At the same time, however, such a ruling should never be enforced to the extent of possibly hampering a viewer's understanding, enjoyment and general involvement. It is also somewhat presumptuous to claim that any production of a Shakespeare play is in any way 'definitive' or 'orthodox', or indeed anything other than an individual interpretation of the work as written. Shakespeare's genius is far too wide-ranging to be 'caught' in one go; all any director can hope to do is to bring out certain aspects of a play, often to the exclusion of others, and it is the director's right, as the interpreter of a work of genius, to be allowed to do so. If omissions, and even rearrangements, have to be made in order to facilitate a director's attempt to tell the play's story, and to ensure an audience's involvement, then they have to be made. Sometimes, too, we have allowed an actor, in consultation with the director, to use a version of the text other than

Professor Alexander's at certain points in the play, if he or she has felt that the performance is thereby improved.

In the television production of *The Taming of the Shrew* Jonathan Miller and I decided after considerable discussion to omit the whole of that curious, lengthy and disappointingly unresolved opening known as 'the Induction'. We made this decision for the following reasons: firstly, because we felt that it may confuse the viewer coming to the play for the first time, very possibly to the detriment of his enjoyment of the play as a whole; secondly, because it is an essentially theatrical device which, while it has been known to work well in a theatre before a live audience, would not come across successfully in the very different medium of television; and lastly, because it is a device which presents the play's characters as 'actors', and we felt that this would hinder the attempt, in this production, to present them as real people in a real, and ultimately quite serious, situation.

Apart from the exclusion of the Induction and a few other small excisions and changes, the production remains faithful to the text as printed here, which is presented in its entirety. For those who wish to compare the text with the television production, all cuts and changes are referred to in the right-hand margin, and in addition the cuts are marked by vertical lines on either side of the text. Marginal notes also include anything that might have been added to aid the business of telling the story, and any stage directions which differ markedly from those in the text. Scene-divisions are presented in the margin as they were in the camera-script which was prepared for production, and are numbered accordingly (sometimes a single television scene may include more than one of the textual scenes). No mention, however, has been made of the common television practice of allowing characters to be 'discovered' at the start of a scene rather than making them enter it, and of cutting away from a scene before anyone has left, even though the printed text begins each scene with the word 'enter' and ends it with 'exit' or 'exeunt'. Neither have I mentioned the occasional alteration to the text which is *not* deliberate, and which is in any case entirely due to the pressures of a television studio. When a scene can only be recorded three or four times at the most, the version that is finally used must always be the one that is best in terms of performance rather than complete textual accuracy; and even the finest actors are capable of unwittingly substituting a 'but' for an 'and', or a 'thou' for a 'you' – and indeed of committing even harsher sins at the last moment!

DAVID SNODIN

30

THE TAMING OF THE SHREW

DRAMATIS PERSONÆ

*A LORD,
*CHRISTOPHER tinker, } *Persons in the Induction.*
*HOSTESS, PAGE, PLAYERS, HUNTSMEN, SERVANTS.

BAPTISTA MINOLA, *a gentleman of Padua.*
VINCENTIO, *a merchant of Pisa.*
LUCENTIO, *son to Vincentio, in love with Bianca.*
PETRUCHIO, *a gentleman of Verona, a suitor to Katherina.*
GREMIO,
HORTENSIO, } *suitors to Bianca.*

TRANIO,
BIONDELLO, } *servants to Lucentio.*
GRUMIO,
CURTIS, } *servants to Petruchio.*
A PEDANT.
KATHERINA, *the shrew,*
BIANCA, } *daughters to Bapista.*
A WIDOW.
TAILOR, HABERDASHER, *and* SERVANTS *attending on Baptista and Petruchio.*

*In the television production the 'Persons in the Induction' are omitted.

THE SCENE : *Padua, and Petruchio's house in the country.*

INDUCTION.

SCENE I. *Before an alehouse on a heath.*

Enter HOSTESS *and* SLY.

Induction omitted.

SLY. I'll pheeze you, in faith.
HOST. A pair of stocks, you rogue !
SLY. Y'are a baggage ; the Slys are no rogues. Look in the chronicles : we came in with Richard Conqueror. Therefore, paucas pallabris ; let the world slide Sessa !   5
HOST. You will not pay for the glasses you have burst ?
SLY. No, not a denier. Go by, Saint Jeronimy, go to thy cold bed and warm thee.
HOST. I know my remedy ; I must go fetch the thirdborough. [*exit.*
SLY. Third, or fourth, or fifth borough, I'll answer him by law. I'll not budge an inch, boy ; let him come, and kindly.
          [*falls asleep.*

Wind horns. Enter a LORD *from hunting, with his* TRAIN.

LORD. Huntsman, I charge thee, tender well my hounds ;
Brach Merriman, the poor cur, is emboss'd ;   15
And couple Clowder with the deep-mouth'd brach.
Saw'st thou not, boy, how Silver made it good
At the hedge corner, in the coldest fault ?
I would not lose the dog for twenty pound.
I HUN. Why, Belman is as good as he, my lord ;   20

Induction omitted.

He cried upon it at the merest loss,
And twice to-day pick'd out the dullest scent;
Trust me, I take him for the better dog.
LORD. Thou art a fool : If Echo were as fleet,
I would esteem him worth a dozen such.   25
But sup them well, and look unto them all;
To-morrow I intend to hunt again.
1 HUN. I will, my lord.
LORD. What's here ? One dead, or drunk ?
See, doth he breathe ?
2 HUN. He breathes, my lord.   Were he not warm'd with ale,   30
This were a bed but cold to sleep so soundly.
LORD O monstrous beast, how like a swine he lies !
Grim death, how foul and loathsome is thine image !
Sirs, I will practise on this drunken man.
What think you, if he were convey'd to bed,   35
Wrapp'd in sweet clothes, rings put upon his fingers,
A most delicious banquet by his bed,
And brave attendants near him when he wakes,
Would not the beggar then forget himself ?
1 HUN. Believe me, lord, I think he cannot choose.   40
2 HUN. It would seem strange unto him when he wak'd.
LORD. Even as a flatt'ring dream or worthless fancy.
Then take him up, and manage well the jest :
Carry him gently to my fairest chamber,
And hang it round with all my wanton pictures ;   45
Balm his foul head in warm distilled waters,
And burn sweet wood to make the lodging sweet;
Procure me music ready when he wakes,
To make a dulcet and a heavenly sound ;
And if he chance to speak, be ready straight,   50
And with a low submissive reverence
Say ' What is it your honour will command ? '
Let one attend him with a silver basin
Full of rose-water and bestrew'd with flowers ·
Another bear the ewer, the third a diaper,   55
And say ' Will't please your lordship cool your hands ? '
Some one be ready with a costly suit,
And ask him what apparel he will wear ;
Another tell him of his hounds and horse,
And that his lady mourns at his disease ;   60
Persuade him that he hath been lunatic,
And, when he says he is, say that he dreams,
For he is nothing but a mighty lord.
This do, and do it kindly, gentle sirs ;
It will be pastime passing excellent,   65
If it be husbanded with modesty.
1 HUN. My lord, I warrant you we will play our part
As he shall think by our true diligence
He is no less than what we say he is.
LORD. Take him up gently, and to bed with him ;   70
And each one to his office when he wakes.
                    [Sly is carried out.   A trumpet sounds.
Sirrah, go see what trumpet 'tis that sounds—   [exit Servant.

32

Belike some noble gentleman that means,
Travelling some journey, to repose him here.

Re-enter a SERVINGMAN

How now ! who is it ?
SERV.   An't please your honour, players   75
    That offer service to your lordship.
LORD. Bid them come near.

Enter PLAYERS.

                    Now, fellows, you are welcome.
PLAYERS. We thank your honour.
LORD. Do you intend to stay with me to-night ?
PLAYER. So please your lordship to accept our duty.   80
LORD With all my heart.   This fellow I remember
    Since once he play'd a farmer's eldest son ;
    'Twas where you woo'd the gentlewoman so well.
    I have forgot your name ; but, sure, that part
    Was aptly fitted and naturally perform'd.   85
PLAYER. I think 'twas Soto that your honour means.
LORD.   'Tis very true; thou didst it excellent.
    Well, you are come to me in happy time,
    The rather for I have some sport in hand
    Wherein your cunning can assist me much.   90
    There is a lord will hear you play to-night ;
    But I am doubtful of your modesties,
    Lest, over-eying of his odd behaviour,
    For yet his honour never heard a play,
    You break into some merry passion   95
    And so offend him ; for I tell you, sirs,
    If you should smile, he grows impatient.
PLAYER. Fear not, my lord ; we can contain ourselves,
    Were he the veriest antic in the world.
LORD. Go, sirrah, take them to the buttery,   100
    And give them friendly welcome every one ;
    Let them want nothing that my house affords.
                                  [*exit one with the* PLAYERS.
    Sirrah, go you to Barthol'mew my page,
    And see him dress'd in all suits like a lady ;
    That done, conduct him to the drunkard's chamber,   105
    And call him ' madam ', do him obeisance.
    Tell him from me—as he will win my love—
    He bear himself with honourable action,
    Such as he hath observ'd in noble ladies
    Unto their lords, by them accomplished ;   110
    Such duty to the drunkard let him do,
    With soft low tongue and lowly courtesy,
    And say ' What is't your honour will command,
    Wherein your lady and your humble wife
    May show her duty and make known her love ? '   115
    And then with kind embracements, tempting kisses,
    And with declining head into his bosom,
    Bid him shed tears, as being overjoyed
    To see her noble lord restor'd to health,

Who for this seven years hath esteemed him   120 | Induction omitted.
No better than a poor and loathsome beggar.
And if the boy have not a woman's gift
To rain a shower of commanded tears,
An onion will do well for such a shift,
Which, in a napkin being close convey'd,   125
Shall in despite enforce a watery eye.
See this dispatch'd with all the haste thou canst ;
Anon I'll give thee more instructions.   [exit a SERVINGMAN.
I know the boy will well usurp the grace,
Voice. gait, and action, of a gentlewoman ;   130
I long to hear him call the drunkard ' husband ' :
And how my men will stay themselves from laughter
When they do homage to this simple peasant.
I'll in to counsel them ; haply my presence
May well abate the over-merry spleen,   135
Which otherwise would grow into extremes.   [exeunt.

SCENE II. *A bedchamber in the Lord's house.*

Enter aloft SLY, *with* ATTENDANTS ; *some with apparel, basin and
ewer, and other appurtenances ; and* LORD.

SLY. For God's sake, a pot of small ale.
1 SERV. Will't please your lordship drink a cup of sack ?
2 SERV. Will't please your honour taste of these conserves ?
3 SERV. What raiment will your honour wear to-day ?
SLY. I am Christophero Sly , call not me honour nor ' lordship '.
    I ne'er drank sack in my life ; and if you give me any conserves,
    give me conserves o' beef. Ne'er ask me what raiment I'll wear,
    for I have no more doublets than backs, no more stockings than
    legs, nor no more shoes than feet—nay, sometime more feet than
    shoes, or such shoes as my toes look through the overleather. 11
LORD. Heaven cease this die humour in your honour !
    O, that a mighty man of such descent,
    Of such possessions, and so high esteem,
    Should be infused with so foul a spirit !   15
SLY. What, would you make me mad ? Am not I Christopher Sly,
    old Sly's son of Burton Heath ; by birth a pedlar, by education a
    cardmaker, by transmutation a bear-herd, and now by present
    profession a tinker. Ask Marian Hacket the fat ale-wife of
    Wincot, if she know me not ; if she say I am not fourteen pence
    on the score for sheer ale. score me up for the lying'st knave in
    Christendom. What . I am not bestraught. [*taking a pot of ale.*]
    Here's—   23
3 SERV. O this it is that makes your lady mourn !
2 SERV. O this is it that makes your servants droop !
LORD. Hence comes it that your kindred shuns your house,
    As beaten hence by your strange lunacy.
    O noble lord, bethink thee of thy birth !
    Call home thy ancient thoughts from banishment,
    And banish hence these abject owly dreams.   30
    Look how thy servants do attend on thee,
    Each in his office ready at thy beck.
    Wilt thou have music ? Hark ! Apollo plays,   [*music.*

And twenty caged nightingales do sing.
Or wilt thou sleep ?   We'll have thee to a couch   35
Softer and sweeter than the lustful bed
On purpose trimm'd up for Semiramis.
Say thou wilt walk : we will bestrew the ground.
Or wilt thou ride ?   Thy horses shall be trapp d,
Their harness studded all with gold and pearl.   40
Dost thou love hawking ?   Thou hast hawks will soar
Above the morning lark.   Or wilt thou hunt ?
Thy hounds shall make the welkin answer them
And fetch shrill echoes from the hollow earth.

1 SERV. Say thou wilt course , thy greyhounds are as swift   45
As breathed stags ; ay, fleeter than the roe.

2 SERV. Dost thou love pictures ?   We will fetch thee straight
Adonis painted by a running brook,
And Cytherea all in sedges hid,
Which seem to move and wanton with her breath   50
Even as the waving sedges play wi' th' wind.

LORD. We'll show thee Io as she was a maid
And how she was beguiled and surpris'd,
As lively painted as the deed was done.

3 SERV. Or Daphne roaming through a thorny wood,   55
Scratching her legs, that one shall swear she bleeds
And at that sight shall sad Apollo weep,
So workmanly the blood and tears are drawn.

LORD. Thou art a lord, and nothing but a lord.
Thou hast a lady far more beautiful   60
Than any woman in this waning age.

1 SERV. And, till the tears that she hath shed for thee
Like envious floods o'er-run her lovely face,
She was the fairest creature in the world ;
And yet she is inferior to none.   65

SLY. Am I a lord and have I such a lady ?
Or do I dream ?   Or have I dream'd till now ?
I do not sleep : I see, I hear, I speak ;
I smell sweet savours, and I feel soft things.
Upon my life, I am a lord indeed,   70
And not a tinker, nor Christopher Sly.
Well, bring our lady hither to our sight ;
And once again, a pot o' th' smallest ale.

2 SERV. Will't please your Mightiness to wash your hands ?
O, how we joy to see your wit restor'd !   75
O, that once more you knew but what you are !
These fifteen years you have been in a dream ;
Or, when you wak'd, so wak'd as if you slept.

SLY. These fifteen years ! by my fay, a goodly nap.
But did I never speak of all that time ?   80

1 SERV. O, yes, my lord, but very idle words ;
For though you lay here in this goodly chamber,
Yet would you say ye were beaten out of door ;
And rail upon the hostess of the house,
And say you would present her at the leet,   85
Because she brought stone jugs and no seal'd quarts.
Sometimes you would call out for Cicely Hacket.

Induction omitted.

SLY. Ay, the woman's maid of the house.
3 SERV. Why, sir, you know no house nor no such maid,
   Nor no such men as you have reckon'd up,   90
   As Stephen Sly, and old John Naps of Greece,
   And Peter Turph, and Henry Pimpernell ;
   And twenty more such names and men as these,
   Which never were, nor no man ever saw.
SLY. Now, Lord be thanked for my good amends !   95
ALL. Amen.

      Enter the PAGE *as a lady, with* ATTENDANTS.

SLY. I thank thee ; thou shalt not lose by it.
PAGE. How fares my noble lord ?
SLY. Marry, I fare well ; for here is cheer enough.
   Where is my wife ?   100
PAGE. Here, noble lord ; what is thy will with her ?
SLY. Are you my wife, and will not call me husband ?
   My men should call me ' lord ' ; I am your goodman.
PAGE. My husband and my lord, my lord and husband ;
   I am your wife in all obedience.   105
SLY. I know it well. What must I call her ?
LORD.   Madam.
SLY. Al'ce madam, or Joan madam ?
LORD. Madam, and nothing else ; so lords call ladies.
SLY. Madam wife, they say that I have dream'd   110
   And slept above some fifteen year or more.
PAGE. Ay, and the time seems thirty unto me,
   Being all this time abandon'd from your bed.
SLY. 'Tis much. Servants, leave me and her alone.
                    [exeunt SERVANTS.
   Madam, undress you, and come now to bed.   115
PAGE. Thrice noble lord, let me entreat of you
   To pardon me yet for a night or two ;
   Or, if not so, until the sun be set.
   For your physicians have expressly charg'd,
   In peril to incur your former malady,   120
   That I should yet absent me from your bed.
   I hope this reason stands for my excuse.
SLY. Ay, it stands so that I may hardly tarry so long. But I would
   be loath to fall into my dreams again. I will therefore tarry in
   despite of the flesh and the blood.   125

          Enter a MESSENGER.

MESS. Your honour's players, hearing your amendment,
   Are come to play a pleasant comedy ;
   For so your doctors hold it very meet,
   Seeing too much sadness hath congeal'd your blood,
   And melancholy is the nurse of frenzy.   130
   Therefore they thought it good you hear a play
   And frame your mind to mirth and merriment,
   Which bars a thousand harms and lengthens life.
SLY. Marry, I will ; let them play it.   Is not a comonty a Christmas
   gambold or a tumbling-trick ?   135
PAGE. No, my good lord, it is more pleasing stuff.

Induction omitted.

36

SLY. What, household stuff?
PAGE. It is a kind of history.
SLY. Well, we'll see't. Come, madam wife, sit by my side and let
   the world slip . we shall ne'er be younger.   *[they sit down.*
       A flourish of trumpets announces the play.

Induction omitted.

ACT ONE.

SCENE I. *Padua. A public place.*

Enter LUCENTIO *and his man* TRANIO.

LUC. Tranio, since for the great desire I had
   To see fair Padua, nursery of arts,
   I am arriv'd for fruitful Lombardy,
   The pleasant garden of great Italy,
   And by my father's love and leave am arm'd   5
   With his good will and thy good company,
   My trusty servant well approv'd in all,
   Here let us breathe, and haply institute
   A course of learning and ingenious studies.
   Pisa, renowned for grave citizens,   10
   Gave me my being and my father first,
   A merchant of great traffic through the world,
   Vincentio, come of the Bentivolii ;
   Vincentio's son, brought up in Florence,
   It shall become to serve all hopes conceiv'd,   15
   To deck his fortune with his virtuous deeds.
   And therefore, Tranio, for the time I study,
   Virtue and that part of philosophy
   Will I apply that treats of happiness
   By virtue specially to be achiev'd.   20
   Tell me thy mind ; for I have Pisa left
   And am to Padua come as he that leaves
   A shallow plash to plunge him in the deep,
   And with satiety seeks to quench his thirst.
TRA. Mi perdonato, gentle master mine   25
   I am in all affected as yourself
   Glad that you thus continue your resolve
   To suck the sweets of sweet philosophy.
   Only, good master, while we do admire
   This virtue and this moral discipline,   30
   Let's be no Stoics nor no stocks, I pray,
   Or so devote to Aristotle's checks
   As Ovid be an outcast quite abjur'd.
   Balk logic with acquaintance that you have,
   And practise rhetoric in your common talk ;   35
   Music and poesy use to quicken you ;
   The mathematics and the metaphysics,
   Fall to them as you find your stomach serves you.
   No profit grows where is no pleasure ta'en ;
   In brief, sir, study what you most affect.   40
LUC. Gramercies, Tranio, well dost thou advise.
   If, Biondello, thou wert come ashore,

SCENE I
Exterior. Padua.
A Street. Day.
Various townspeople
– traders, jugglers,
etc. TRANIO and
LUCENTIO enter from
the top of the street.

We could at once put us in readiness,
And take a lodging fit to entertain
Such friends as time in Padua shall beget.   45

Enter BAPTISTA *with his two daughters,* KATHERINA *and* BIANCA;
GREMIO, *a pantaloon,* HORTENSIO, *suitor to* BIANCA. LUCENTIO
and TRANIO *stand by.*

But stay awhile; what company is this?
TRA. Master, some show to welcome us to town.
BAP. Gentlemen, importune me no farther,
    For how I firmly am resolv'd you know;
    That is, not to bestow my youngest daughter   50
    Before I have a husband for the elder.
    If either of you both love Katherina,
    Because I know you well and love you well,
    Leave shall you have to court her at your pleasure.
GRE. To cart her rather. She's too rough for me.   55
    There, there, Hortensio, will you any wife?
KATH. [*to* BAPTISTA.] I pray you, sir, is it your will
    To make a stale of me amongst these mates?
HOR. Mates, maid! How mean you that? No mates for you,
    Unless you were of gentler, milder mould.   60
KATH. I' faith, sir, you shall never need to fear;
    Iwis it is not halfway to her heart;
    But if it were, doubt not her care should be
    To comb your noddle with a three-legg'd stool,
    And paint your face and use you like a fool.   65
HOR. From all such devils, good Lord deliver us!
GRE. And me, too, good Lord!
TRA Husht, master! Here's some good pastime toward
    That wench is stark mad or wonderful froward.
LUC. But in the other's silence do I see   70
    Maid's mild behaviour and sobriety.
    Peace, Tranio!
TRA. Well said, master; mum! and gaze your fill.
BAP. Gentlemen, that I may soon make good
    What I have said—Bianca, get you in;   75
    And let it not displease thee. good Bianca,
    For I will love thee ne'er the less, my girl.
KATH. A pretty peat! it is best
    Put finger in the eye, an she knew why.
BIAN. Sister, content you in my discontent.   80
    Sir, to your pleasure humbly I subscribe;
    My books and instruments shall be my company,
    On them to look, and practise by myself.
LUC. Hark, Tranio, thou mayst hear Minerva speak!
HOR. Signior Baptista, will you be so strange?   85
    Sorry am I that our good will effects
    Bianca's grief.
GRE.   Why will you mew her up,
    Signior Baptista, for this fiend of hell,
    And make her bear the penance of her tongue?
BAP. Gentlemen, content ye; I am resolv'd.   90
    Go in, Bianca.   [*exit* BIANCA.

John Franklyn-Robbins as Baptista, Sarah Badel as Katherina and Susan Penhaligon as Bianca

And for I know she taketh most delight
In music, instruments, and poetry,
Schoolmasters will I keep within my house
Fit to instruct her youth.   If you, Hortensio,   95
Or, Signior Gremio, you, know any such,
Prefer them hither ; for to cunning men
I will be very kind, and liberal
To mine own children in good bringing-up ;
And so, farewell.   Katherina, you may stay ;   100
For I have more to commune with Bianca.   [exit.
KATH. Why, and I trust I may go too, may I not ?
What ! shall I be appointed hours, as though, belike,
I knew not what to take and what to leave ? Ha !
                                                              [exit.
GRE. You may go to the devil's dam ; your gifts are so good here's
none will hold you.   There ! Love is not so great, Hortensio,
but we may blow our nails together, and fast it fairly out ; our
cake's dough on both sides.   Farewell ; yet, for the love I bear
my sweet Bianca, if I can by any means light on a fit man to
teach her that wherein she delights, I will wish him to her father.
HOR. So will I, Signior Gremio ; but a word, I pray.   Though the
nature of our quarrel yet never brook'd parle, know now, upon
advice, it toucheth us both—that we may yet again have access
to our fair mistress, and be happy rivals in Bianca's love—to
labour and effect one thing specially.   116
GRE. What's that, I pray ?
HOR. Marry, sir, to get a husband for her sister.
GRE. A husband ? a devil.
HOR. I say a husband.   120
GRE. I say a devil.   Think'st thou, Hortensio, though her father be
very rich, any man is so very a fool to be married to hell ?
HOR. Tush, Gremio !   Though it pass your patience and mine to
endure her loud alarums, why, man, there be good fellows in the
world, an a man could light on them, would take her with all
faults, and money enough.   127
GRE. I cannot tell ; but I had as lief take her dowry with this condition—to be whipp'd at the high cross every morning.
HOR. Faith, as you say, there's small choice in rotten apples.   But,
come ; since this bar in law makes us friends, it shall be so far
forth friendly maintain'd till by helping Baptista's eldest daughter
to a husband we set his youngest free for a husband, and then
have to't afresh.   Sweet Bianca !   Happy man be his dole !
He that runs fastest gets the ring.   How say you, Signior Gremio ?
GRE. I am agreed ; and would I had given him the best horse in
Padua to begin his wooing that would thoroughly woo her, wed
her, and bed her, and rid the house of her !   Come on.   140
                                 [exeunt GREMIO and HORTENSIO.
TRA. I pray, sir, tell me, is it possible
That love should of a sudden take such hold ?
LUC. O Tranio, till I found it to be true,
I never thought it possible or likely.
But see ! while idly I stood looking on,   145
I found the effect of love in idleness ;
And now in plainness do confess to thee,

That art to me as secret and as dear
As Anna to the Queen of Carthage was—
Tranio, I burn, I pine, I perish, Tranio,   150
If I achieve not this young modest girl.
Counsel me, Tranio, for I know thou canst ;
Assist me, Tranio, for I know thou wilt.
TRA. Master, it is no time to chide you now ·
Affection is not rated from the heart ;   155
It love have touch'd you, nought remains but so :
' Redime te captum quam queas minimo '.
LUC. Gramercies, lad.   Go forward ; this contents ;
The rest will comfort, for thy counsel's sound.
TRA. Master, you look'd so longly on the maid.   160
Perhaps you mark'd not what's the pith of all.
LUC. O, yes, I saw sweet beauty in her face,
Such as the daughter of Agenor had,
That made great Jove to humble him to her hand,
When with his knees he kiss'd the Cretan strand.   165
TRA. Saw you no more ?   Mark'd you not how her sister
Began to scold and raise up such a storm
That mortal ears might hardly endure the din ?
LUC. Tranio, I saw her coral lips to move,
And with her breath she did perfume the air ;   170
Sacred and sweet was all I saw in her.
TRA. Nay, then 'tis time to stir him from his trance.
I pray, awake. sir.   If you love the maid,
Bend thoughts and wits to achieve her.   Thus it stands :
Her elder sister is so curst and shrewd   175
That, till the father rid his hands of her,
Master, your love must live a maid at home ;
And therefore has he closely mew'd her up,
Because she will not be annoy'd with suitors.
LUC. Ah, Tranio, what a cruel father's he !   180
But art thou not advis'd he took some care
To get her cunning schoolmasters to instruct her ?
TRA. Ay, marry, am I, sir, and now 'tis plotted.
LUC. I have it, Tranio.
TRA.   Master, for my hand,
Both our inventions meet and jump in one.   185
LUC. Tell me thine first.
TRA.   You will be schoolmaster,
And undertake the teaching of the maid—
That's your device.
LUC.   It is.   May it be done ?
TRA. Not possible ; for who shall bear your part
And be in Padua here Vincentio's son ;   190
Keep house and ply his book, welcome his friends,
Visit his countrymen, and banquet them ?
LUC. Basta, content thee, for I have it full.
We have not yet been seen in any house,
Nor can we be distinguish'd by our faces   195
For man or master.   Then it follows thus :
Thou shalt be master, Tranio, in my stead,
Keep house and port and servants, as I should ;

I wil some other be—some Florentine,
Some Neapolitan, or meaner man of Pisa.   200
'Tis hatch'd, and shall be so.   Tranio, at once
Uncase thee ; take my colour'd hat and cloak.
When Biondello comes, he waits on thee ;
But I will charm him first to keep his tongue.
TRA. So had you need.   [*they exchange habits.*
    In brief, sir, sith it your pleasure is,   206
    And I am tied to be obedient—
    For so your father charg'd me at our parting :
    ' Be serviceable to my son ' quoth he.
    Although I think 'twas in another sense—   210
    I am content to be Lucentio,
    Because so well I love Lucentio.
LUC. Tranio, be so because Lucentio loves ;
    And let me be a slave t' achieve that maid
    Whose sudden sight hath thrall'd my wounded eye.   215

                Enter BIONDELLO.

    Here comes the rogue.   Sirrah, where have you been ?
BIO. Where have I been !   Nay, how now ! where are you ?
    Master, has my fellow Tranio stol'n your clothes ?
    Or you stol'n his ? or both ?   Pray, what's the news ?
LUC. Sirrah, come hither ; 'tis no time to jest,   220
    And therefore frame your manners to the time.
    Your fellow Tranio here, to save my life,
    Puts my apparel and my count'nance on,
    And I for my escape have put on his ;
    For in a quarrel since I came ashore   225
    I kill'd a man, and fear I was descried.
    Wait you on him, I charge you, as becomes,
    While I make way from hence to save my life.
    You understand me ?
BION.   I, sir ? Ne'er a whit.
LUC. And not a jot of Tranio in your mouth :   230
    Tranio is chang'd into Lucentio.
BION. The better for him , would I were so too !
TRA. So could I, faith, boy, to have the next wish after,
    That Lucentio indeed had Baptista's youngest daughter.
    But, sirrah, not for my sake but your master's, I advise 235
    You use your manners discreetly in all kind of companies.
    When I am alone, why, then I am Tranio ;
    But in all places else your master Lucentio.
LUC. Tranio, let's go.
    One thing more rests, that thyself execute—
    To make one among these wooers.   If thou ask me why—
    Sufficeth, my reasons are both good and weighty.   [*exeunt.*
            The Presenters above speak.
I SERV. My lord, you nod ; you do not mind the play.   242
SLY Yes, by Saint Anne do I.   A good matter, surely ; comes there
    any more of it ?
PAGE. My lord, 'tis but begun.   245
SLY. 'Tis a very excellent piece of work, madam lady.   Would
    'twere done !   [*they sit and mark.*

LUCENTIO, TRANIO
and BIONDELLO leave,
passing PETRUCHIO
and GRUMIO
entering.

Lines 242–247
omitted.

Lucentio (Simon Chandler), Biondello (Harry Waters), an extra and Tranio (Anthony Pedley)

SCENE II. *Padua. Before Hortensio's house.*

Enter PETRUCHIO *and his man* GRUMIO.

No change of scene.
Scene I continues.

PET. Verona, for a while I take my leave,
To see my friends in Padua ; but of all
My best beloved and approved friend,
Hortensio ; and I trow this is his house.
Here, sirrah Grumio, knock, I say.   5
GRU. Knock, sir ! Whom should I knock ?
Is there any man has rebus'd your worship ?
PET. Villian, I say, knock me here soundly.
GRU. Knock you here, sir ? Why, sir, what am I, sir, that I should
knock you here, sir ?
PET. Villian, I say, knock me at this gate,
And rap me well, or I'll knock your knave's pate.
GRU. My master is grown quarrelsome. I should knock you first,
And then I know after who comes by the worst.   15
PET. Will it not be ?
Faith, sirrah, an you'll not knock I'll ring it ;
I'll try how you can sol-fa, and sing it.
                                        [*he wrings him by the ears.*
GRU. Help, masters, help ! My master is mad.
PET. Now knock when I bid you, sirrah villian !

Enter HORTENSIO.

HOR. How now ! what's the matter ? My old friend Grumio and
my good friend Petruchio ! How do you all at Verona ?   22
PET. Signior Hortensio, come you to part the fray ?
' Con tutto il cuore ben trovato ' may I say.
HOR. Alla nostra casa ben venuto,
Molto honorato signor mio Petrucio.
Rise, Grumio, rise ; we will compound this quarrel.
GRU. Nay, 'tis no matter, sir, what he 'leges in Latin. If this be not
a lawful cause for me to leave his service—look you, sir : he bid
me knock him and rap him soundly, 'sir. Well, was it fit for a
servant to use his master so ; being, perhaps, for aught I see,
two and thirty, a pip out ?   32
Whom would to God I had well knock'd at first,
Then had not Grumio come by the worst.
PET. A senseless villain ! Good Hortensio,
I bade the rascal knock upon your gate,
And could not get him for my heart to do it.
GRU. Knock at the gate ? O heavens ! Spake you not these words
plain : ' Sirrah knock me here, rap me here, knock me well, and
knock me soundly ' ? And come you now with ' knocking at the
gate ' ?   41
PET. Sirrah, be gone, or talk not, I advise you.
HOR. Petruchio, patience ; I am Grumio's pledge ;
Why, this's a heavy chance 'twixt him and you,
Your ancient, trusty, pleasant servant Grumio.   45
And tell me now, sweet friend, what happy gale
Blows you to Padua here from old Verona ?
PET. Such wind as scatters young men through the world
To seek their fortunes farther than at home,

Where small experience grows.   But in a few,   50
Signior Hortensio, thus it stands with me :
Antonio, my father, is deceas'd,
And I have thrust myself into this maze,
Haply to wive and thrive as best I may ;
Crowns in my purse I have, and goods at home,   55
And so am come abroad to see the world.

HOR. Petruchio, shall I then come roundly to thee
And wish thee to a shrewd ill-favour'd wife ?
Thou'dst thank me but a little for my counsel,
And yet I'll promise thee she shall be rich,   60
And very rich ; but th'art too much my friend,
And I'll not wish thee to her.

PET. Signior Hortensio, 'twixt such friends as we
Few words suffice ; and therefore, if thou know
One rich enough to be Petruchio's wife,   65
As wealth is burden of my wooing dance,
Be she as foul as was Florentius' love,
As old as Sibyl, and as curst and shrewd
As Socrates' Xanthippe or a worse—
She moves me not, or not removes, at least,   70
Affection's edge in me, were she as rough
As are the swelling Adriatic seas.
I come to wive it wealthily in Padua ;
If wealthily, then happily in Padua.   74

GRU. Nay, look you, sir, he tells you flatly what his mind is.   Why,
give him gold enough and marry him to a puppet or an aglet-baby,
or an old trot with ne'er a tooth in her head, though she have as
many diseases as two and fifty horses.   Why, nothing comes
amiss, so money comes withal.   80

HOR. Petruchio, since we are stepp'd thus far in,
I will continue that I broach'd in jest.
I can, Petruchio, help thee to a wife
With wealth enough, and young and beauteous ;
Brought up as best becomes a gentlewoman ;   85
Her only fault, and that is faults enough,
Is—that she is intolerable curst,
And shrewd and froward so beyond all measure
That, were my state far worser than it is,
I would not wed her for a mine of gold.   90

PET. Hortensio, peace ! thou know'st not gold's effect.
Tell me her father's name, and 'tis enough ;
For I will board her though she chide as loud
As thunder when the clouds in autumn crack.

HOR. Her father is Baptista Minola,   95
An affable and courteous gentleman ;
Her name is Katherina Minola,
Renown'd in Padua for her scolding tongue.

PET. I know her father, though I know not her ;
And he knew my deceased father well.   100
I will not sleep, Hortensio, till I see her ;
And therefore let me be thus bold with you
To give you over at this first encounter,
Unless you will accompany me thither.   104

GRU. I pray you, sir, let him go while the humour lasts. O' my word, an she knew him as well as I do, she would think scolding would do little good upon him. She may perhaps call him half a score knaves or so. Why, that's nothing; an he begin once, he'll rail in his rope-tricks. I'll tell you what, sir : an she stand him but a little, he will throw a figure in her face, and so disfigure her with it that she shall have no more eyes to see withal than a cat. You know him not, sir. 113

HOR. Tarry, Petruchio, I must go with thee,
For in Baptista's keep my treasure is. 115
He hath the jewel of my life in hold,
His youngest daughter, beautiful Bianca ;
And her withholds from me, and other more,
Suitors to her and rivals in my love ;
Supposing it a thing impossible— 120
For those defects I have before rehears'd—
That ever Katherina will be woo'd.
Therefore this order hath Baptista ta'en,
That none shall have access unto Bianca
Till Katherine the curst have got a husband. 125

GRU. Katherine the curst !
A title for a maid of all titles the worst.

HOR. Now shall my friend Petruchio do me grace,
And offer me disguis'd in sober robes
To old Baptista as a schoolmaster 130
Well seen in music. to instruct Bianca ;
That so I may by this device at least
Have leave and leisure to make love to her,
And unsuspected court her by herself.

Enter GREMIO *with* LUCENTIO *disguised as* CAMBIO.

GRU. Here's no knavery ! See, to beguile the old folks, how the young folks lay their heads together ! Master, master, look about you. Who goes there, ha ? 137

HOR. Peace, Grumio ! It is the rival of my love. Petruchio, stand by awhile.

GRU. A proper stripling, and an amorous ! *[they stand aside.*

GRE. O, very well ; I have perus'd the note.
Hark you, sir ; I'll have them very fairly bound—
All books of love, see that at any hand ;
And see you read no other lectures to her.
You understand me—over and beside 145
Signior Baptista's liberality,
I'll mend it with a largess. Take your paper too,
And let me have them very well perfum'd ;
For she is sweeter than perfume itself
To whom they go to. What will you read to her ? 150

LUC. Whate'er I read to her, I'll plead for you
As for my patron, stand you so assur'd,
As firmly as yourself were still in place ;
Yea, and perhaps with more successful words
Than you, unless you were a scholar, sir. 155

GRE. O this learning, what a thing it is !

GRU. O this woodcock, what an ass it is !

PET. Peace, sirrah!
HOR. Grumio, mum! [*coming forward.*]
    God save you. Signior Gremio!
GRE. And you are well met, Signior Hortensio.   160
    Trow you whither I am going?   To Baptista Minola.
    I promis'd to enquire carefully
    About a schoolmaster for the fair Bianca;
    And by good fortune I have lighted well
    On this young man; for learning and behaviour   165
    Fit for her turn, well read in poetry
    And other books—good ones, I warrant ye.
HOR. 'Tis well; and I have met a gentleman
    Hath promis'd me to help me to another,
    A fine musician to instruct our mistress;   170
    So shall I no whit be behind in duty
    To fair Bianca, so beloved of me.
GRE. Beloved of me—and that my deeds shall prove.
GRU. And that his bags shall prove.
HOR. Gremio, 'tis now no time to vent our love.   175
    Listen to me, and if you speak me fair
    I'll tell you news indifferent good for either.
    Here is a gentleman whom by chance I met,
    Upon agreement from us to his liking,
    Will undertake to woo curst Katherine;   180
    Yea, and to marry her, if her dowry please.
GRE. So said. so done, is well.
    Hortensio, have you told him all her faults?
PET. I know she is an irksome brawling scold;
    If that be all, masters, I hear no harm.   185
GRE, No, say'st me so, friend?   What countryman?
PET. Born in Verona, old Antonio's son.
    My father dead, my fortune lives for me;
    And I do hope good days and long to see.
GRE. O sir, such a life with such a wife were strange!   190
    But if you have a stomach, to't a God's name;
    You shall have me assisting you in all.
    But will you woo this wild-cat?
PET.   Will I live?
GRU. Will he woo her?   Ay, or I'll hang her.
PET. Why came I hither but to that intent?   195
    Think you a little din can daunt mine ears?
    Have I not in my time heard lions roar?
    Have I not heard the sea, puff'd up with winds,
    Rage like an angry boar chafed with sweat?
    Have I not heard great ordnance in the field,   200
    And heaven's artillery thunder in the skies?
    Have I not in a pitched battle heard
    Loud 'larums, neighing steeds, and trumpets' clang?
    And do you tell me of a woman's tongue,
    That gives not half so great a blow to hear   205
    As will a chestnut in a farmer's fire?
    Tush! tush! fear boys with bugs.
GRU.   For he fears none.
GRE. Hortensio, hark:

TRANIO and
BIONDELLO appear at
the top of the street.

This gentleman is happily arriv'd,
My mind presumes, for his own good and ours.   210
HOR. I promis'd we would be contributors
And bear his charge of wooing, whatsoe'er.
GRE. And so we will—prov ded that he win her.
GRU. I would I were as sure of a good dinner.

Enter TRANIO, *bravely apparelled as* LUCENTIO, *and* BIONDELLO.

TRA. Gentlemen, God save you ! If I may be bold,   215
Tell me, I beseech you, which is the readiest way
To the house of Signior Baptista Minola ?
BION. He that has the two fair daughters ; is't he you mean ?
TRA. Even he, Biondello.   220
GRE. Hark you, sir, you mean not her to—
TRA. Perhaps him and her, sir . what have you to do ?
PET. Not her that chides, sir, at ny hand, I pray.
TRA. I love no chiders, sir.   Biondello, let's away.
LUC. [*aside.*] Well begun, Tranio.
HOR.   Sir, a word ere you go.   225
Are you a suitor to the maid you talk of, yea or no ?
TRA. And if I be, sir. is it any offence ?
GRE. No ; if without more words you will get you hence.
TRA. Why, sir, I pray, are not the streets as free
For me as for you ?
GRE.   But so is not she.   230
TRA. For what reason, I beseech you ?
GRE. For this reason, if you'll know,
Tha she's the choice love of Signior Gremio.
HOR. That she's the chosen of Signior Hortensio.
TRA. Softly, my masters ! If you be gentlemen,
Do me this right—hear me with patience.   235
Baptista is a noble gentleman,
To whom my father is not all unknown,
And, were his daughter fairer than she is,
She may more suitors have, and me for one.
Fair Leda's daughter had a thousand wooers ;   240
Then well one more may fair Bianca have ,
And so she shall : Lucentio shall make one,
Though Paris came in hope to speed alone.
GRE. What, this gentleman will out-talk us al !
LUC. Sir, give him head ; I know he'll prove a jade.   245
PET. Hortensio, to what end are all these words ?
HOR. Sir let me be so bold as ask you.
Did you yet ever see Baptista's daughter ?
TRA. No, sir, but hear I do that he hath two :
The one as famous for a scolding tongue   250
As is the other for beauteous modesty.
PET. Sir, sir, the first's for me , let her go by.
GRE. Yea, leave that labour to great Hercules,
And let it be more than Alcides' twelve.
PET. Sir, understand you this of me, in sooth :   255
The youngest daughter, whom you hearken for,
Her father keeps from all access of suitors,
And will not promise her to any man

Sarah Badel as Katherina and Susan Penhaligon as Bianca

Petruchio and Katherina (John Cleese and Sarah Badel) with Baptista (John Franklyn-Robbins)

Baptista (John Franklyn-Robbins), Tranio (Anthony Pedley) and Petruchio (John Cleese)

Sarah Badel as Katherina

Sarah Badel and John Cleese as
Katherina and Petruchio

Jonathan Cecil and Frank Thornton as
Hortensio and Gremio

Petruchio and Katherina with their servants, including Grumio (David Kincaid, with
hat)

Sarah Badel as Katherina

Susan Penhaligon as Bianca and Simon Chandler as Lucentio

Until the elder sister first be wed.
The younger then is free, and not before.   260
TRA. If it be so, sir, that you are the man
   Must stead us all, and me amongst the rest;
   And if you break the ice, and do this feat,
   Achieve the elder, set the younger free
   For our access—whose hap shall be to have her   265
   Will not so graceless be to be ingrate.
HOR. Sir, you say well, and well you do conceive,
   And since you do profess to be a suitor,
   You must, as we do, gratify this gentleman,
   To whom we all rest generally beholding.   270
TRA. Sir, I shall not be slack; in sign whereof,
   Please ye we may contrive this afternoon,
   And quaff carouses to our mistress' health;
   And do as adversaries do in law—
   Strive mightily, but eat and drink as friends.   275
GRU., BION. O excellent motion! Fellows, let's be gone.
HOR. The motion's good indeed, and be it so.
   Petruchio, I shall be your ben venuto.   [exeunt.

ACT TWO.

SCENE I. *Padua. Baptista's house.*

Enter KATHERINA *and* BIANCA.

BIAN. Good sister, wrong me not, nor wrong yourself,
   To make a bondmaid and a slave of me—
   That I disdain; but for these other gawds,
   Unbind my hands, I'll pull them off myself,
   Yea, all my raiment, to my petticoat;   5
   Or what you will command me will I do,
   So well I know my duty to my elders.
KATH. Of all thy suitors here I charge thee tell
   Whom thou lov'st best. See thou dissemble not.
BIAN. Believe me, sister, of all the men alive   10
   I never yet beheld that special face
   Which I could fancy more than any other.
KATH. Minion, thou liest. Is't not Hortensio?
BIAN. If you affect him, sister, here I swear
   I'll plead for you myself but you shall have him.   15
KATH. O then, belike, you fancy riches more:
   You will have Gremio to keep you fair.
BIAN. Is it for him you do envy me so?
   Nay, then you jest; and now I well perceive
   You have but jested with me all this while.   20
   I prithee, sister Kate, untie my hands.
KATH. [*strikes her.*] If that be jest, then all the rest was so.

Enter BAPTISTA.

BAP. Why, how now, dame! Whence grows this insolence?
   Bianca, stand aside—poor girl! she weeps.   [*he unbinds her.*
   Go ply thy needle; meddle not with her.   25

SCENE 2
*Interior. Baptista's
House. Day.*
A female Servant is
sweeping.
KATHERINA and
BIANCA appear
through a doorway,
BIANCA with her
hands tied.

For shame, thou hilding of a devilish spirit,
Why dost thou wrong her that did ne'er wrong thee ?
When did she cross thee with a bitter word ?
KATH. Her silence flouts me, and I'll be reveng'd.
[flies after BIANCA.
BAP. What, in my sight ? Bianca, get thee in. *[exit* BIANCA.
KATH. What, will you not suffer me ? Nay, now I see
She is your treasure, she must have a husband ;
I must dance bare-foot on her wedding-day,
And for your love to her lead apes in hell.
Talk not to me ; I will go sit and weep,   35
Till I can find occasion of revenge.   *[exit* KATHERINA.
BAP. Was ever gentleman thus griev'd as I ?
But who comes here ?
Enter GREMIO, *with* LUCENTIO *in the habit of a mean man ;* PETRUCHIO,
with HORTENSIO *as a musician ; and* TRANIO, *as* LUCENTIO, *with his
boy,* BIONDELLO, *bearing a lute and books.*
GRE. Good morrow, neighbour Baptista.   39
BAP. Good morrow, neighbour Gremio.
God save you, gentlemen !
PET. And you, good sir ! Pray, have you not a daughter
Call'd Katherina, fair and virtuous ?
BAP. I have a daughter, sir, call'd Katherina.
GRE. You are too blunt ; go to it orderly.   45
PET. You wrong me, Signior Gremio ; give me leave.
I am a gentleman of Verona, sir.
That, hearing of her beauty and her wit,
Her affability and bashful modesty,
Her wondrous qualities and mild behaviour,   50
Am bold to show myself a forward guest
Within your house, to make mine eye the witness
Of that report which I so oft have heard.
And, for an entrance to my entertainment,
I do present you with a man of mine,   *[presenting* HORTENSIO.
Cunning in music and the mathematics,
To instruct her fully in those sciences,
Whereof I know she is not ignorant.
Accept of him, or else you do me wrong—
His name is Licio, born in Mantua.   60
BAP. Y'are welcome, sir, and he for your good sake.
But for my daughter Katherine, this I know,
She is not for your turn, the more my grief.
PET I see you do not mean to part with her ;
Or else you like not of my company.   65
BAP. Mistake me not ; I speak but as I find.
Whence are you, sir ? What may I call your name ?
PET. Petruchio is my name, Antonio's son,
A man well known throughout all Italy.
BAP. I know him well ; you are welcome for his sake.   70
GRE. Saving your tale, Petruchio, I pray,
Let us that are poor petitioners speak too.
Bacare ! you are marvellous forward.
PET. O, pardon me, Signior Gremio ! I would fain be doing.
GRE. I doubt it not, sir ; but you will curse your wooing.   75

Neighbour, this is a gift very gratetul, I am sure of it.   To express
the like kindness, myselt that have been more kindly beholding
to you than any, treely give unto you this young scholar [*presenting*
LUCENTIO] that hath been long studying at Rheims ; as cunning
in Greek, Latin, and other languages, as the other in music and
mathematics.   His name is Cambio.   Pray accept his service.
BAP. A thousand thanks, Signior Gremio.   Welcome, good Cambio.
[*to* TRANIO.] But, gentle sir, methinks you walk like a stranger.
May I be so bold to know the cause ot your coming ?   86
TRA. Pardon me, sir, the boldness is mine own
    That, being a stranger in this city here.
    Do make myself a suitor to your daughter,
    Unto Bianca, tair and virtuous.   90
    Nor is your firm resolve unknown to me
    In the preterment of the eldest sister.
    This liberty is all that I request—
    That. upon knowledge ot my parentage,
    I may have welcome 'mongst the rest that woo,   95
    And tree access and tavour as the rest.
    And toward the education of your daughters
    I here bestow a simple instrument,
    And this small packet of Greek and Latin books.
    It you accept them. then their worth is great.   100
BAP. Lucentio is your name ?   Ot whence, I pray ?
TRA. Ot Pisa, sir ; son to Vincentio.
BAP. A mighty man ot Pisa.   By report
    I know him well.   You are very welcome, sir.
    Take you the lute, and you the set ot books ;   105
    You shall go see your pupils presently.
    Holla, within !

                  Enter a SERVANT.

                  Sirrah, lead these gentlemen
    To my daughters ; and tell them both
    These are their tutors.   Bid them use them well.
    [*exit* SERVANT *leading* HORTENSIO *carrying the lute and* LUCENTIO
                                              with the books.
    We will go walk a little in the orchard,   110
    And then to dinner.   You are passing welcome,
    And so I pray you all to think yourselves.
PET. Signior Baptista, my business asketh haste,
    And every day I cannot come to woo.
    You knew my father well, and in him me,   115
    Left solely heir to all his lands and goods,
    Which I have bettered rather than decreas'd.
    Then tell me, it I get your daughter's love.
    What dowry shall I have with her to wife ?
BAP. After my death, the one halt ot my lands   120
    And, in possession, twenty thousand crowns.
PET. And tor that dowry, I'l assure her ot
    Her widowhood, be it that she survive me,
    In all my lands and leases whatsoever.
    Let specialities be theretore drawn between us,   125
    That covenants may be kept on either hand.

BAP. Ay, when the special thing is well obtain'd,
　　That is, her love ; for that is all in all.
PET. Why, that is nothing ; for I tell you, father,
　　I am as peremptory as she proud-minded ;　　　　　130
　　And where two raging fires meet together,
　　They do consume the thing that feeds their fury.
　　Though little fire grows great with little wind,
　　Yet extreme gusts will blow out fire and all.
　　So I to her, and so she yields to me ;　　　　　　135
　　For I am rough, and woo not like a babe.
BAP. Well mayst thou woo, and happy be thy speed
　　But be thou arm'd for some unhappy words.
PET. Ay, to the proof, as mountains are for winds,
　　That shake not though they blow perpetually.　　　140

　　　　　Re-enter HORTENSIO, *with his head broke.*

BAP. How now, my friend !　Why dost thou look so pale ?
HOR. For fear, I promise you, if I look pale.
BAP. What, will my daughter prove a good musician ?
HOR. I think she'll sooner prove a soldier :
　　Iron may hold with her, but never lutes.　　　　　145
BAP. Why, then thou canst not break her to the lute ?
HOR. Why, no ; for she hath broke the lute to me.
　　I did but tell her she mistook her frets,
　　And bow'd her hand to teach her fingering,
　　When, with a most impatient devilish spirit,　　　150
　　' Frets, call you these ? ' quoth she ' I'll fume with them '.
　　And with that word she struck me on the head,
　　And through the instrument my pate made way ;
　　And there I stood amazed for a while,
　　As on a pillory, looking through the lute,　　　　155
　　While she did call me rascal fiddler
　　And twangling Jack, with twenty such vile terms,
　　As she had studied to misuse me so.
PET. Now, by the world, it is a lusty wench ;
　　I love her ten times more than e'er I did.　　　　160
　　O, how I long to have some chat with her !
BAP. Well, go with me, and be not so discomfited ;
　　Proceed in practice with my younger daughter ;
　　She's apt to learn, and thankful for good turns.
　　Signior Petruchio, will you go with us,　　　　　165
　　Or shall I send my daughter Kate to you ?
PET. I pray you do.　　　　　　　[*exeunt all but* PETRUCHIO.
　　　　　　　　I'll attend her here,
　　And woo her with some spirit when she comes.
　　Say that she rail ; why, then I'll tell her plain
　　She sings as sweetly as a nightingale.　　　　　170
　　Say that she frown ; I'll say she looks as clear
　　As morning roses newly wash'd with dew.
　　Say she be mute, and will not speak a word ;
　　Then I'll commend her volubility,
　　And say she uttereth piercing eloquence.　　　　175
　　If she do bid me pack, I'll give her thanks,
　　As though she bid me stay by her a week ;

If she deny to wed, I'll crave the day
When I shall ask the banns, and when be married.
But here she comes ; and now, Petruchio, speak.   180

Enter KATHERINA.

Good morrow, Kate—for that's your name, I hear.
KATH. Well have you heard, but something hard of hearing :
  They call me Katherine that do talk of me.
PET. You lie, in faith, for you are call'd plain Kate,
  And bonny Kate, and sometimes Kate the curst ;   185
  But, Kate, the prettiest Kate in Christendom,
  Kate of Kate Hall, my super-dainty Kate,
  For dainties are all Kates, and therefore, Kate,
  Take this of me, Kate of my consolation—
  Hearing thy mildness prais'd in every town,   190
  Thy virtues spoke of, and thy beauty sounded,
  Yet not so deeply as to thee belongs,
  Myself am mov'd to woo thee for my wife.
KATH. Mov'd ! in good time ! Let him that mov'd you hither
  Remove you hence.   I knew you at the first   195
  You were a moveable.
PET.   Why, what's a moveable ?
KATH. A join'd-stool.
PET. Thou hast hit it.   Come, sit on me.
KATH. Asses are made to bear, and so are you.
PET. Women are made to bear, and so are you.
KATH. No such jade as you, if me you mean.   200
PET. Alas, good Kate, I will not burden thee !
  For, knowing thee to be but young and light—
KATH. Too light for such a swain as you to catch ;
  And yet as heavy as my weight should be.
PET. Should be ! should—buzz !
KATH.   Well ta'en, and like a buzzard.   205
PET. O, slow-wing'd turtle, shall a buzzard take thee ?
KATH. Ay, for a turtle, as he takes a buzzard.
PET. Come, come, you wasp ; i' faith, you are too angry.
KATH. If I be waspish, best beware my sting.
PET. My remedy is then to pluck it out.   210
KATH. Ay, if the fool could find it where it lies.
PET. Who knows not where a wasp does wear his sting ?
  In his tail.
KATH. In his tongue.
PET. Whose tongue ?
KATH. Yours, if you talk of tales ; and so farewell.
PET. What, with my tongue in your tail ?   Nay, come again,   215
  Good Kate ; I am a gentleman.
KATH.   That I'll try.   [*she strikes him.*
PET. I swear I'll cuff you, if you strike again.
KATH. So may you lose your arms.
  If you strike me, you are no gentleman ;
  And if no gentleman, why then no arms.   220
PET. A herald, Kate ?   O, put me in thy books !
KATH. What is your crest—a coxcomb ?
PET. A combless cock, so Kate will be my hen.

53

KATH. No cock of mine : you crow too like a craven.
PET. Nay, come, Kate, come ; you must not look so sour.   225
KATH. It is my fashion, when I see a crab.
PET. Why, here's no crab ; and therefore look not sour.
KATH. There is, there is.
PET. Then show it me.
KATH.   Had I a glass I would.
PET. What, you mean my face ?
KATH. Well aim'd of such a young one.   230
PET. Now, by Saint George, I am too young for you.
KATH. Yet you are wither'd.
PET.   'Tis with cares.
KATH.   I care not.
PET. Nay, hear you, Kate—in sooth, you scape not so.
KATH. I chafe you, if I tarry ; let me go.
PET. No, not a whit ; I find you passing gentle.   235
    'Twas told me you were rough, and coy, and sullen,
    And now I find report a very liar ;
    For thou art pleasant, gamesome, passing courteous,
    But slow in speech, yet sweet as springtime flowers.
    Thou canst not frown, thou canst not look askance,   240
    Nor bite the lip, as angry wenches will,
    Nor hast thou pleasure to be cross in talk ;
    But thou with mildness entertain'st thy wooers ;
    With gentle conference, soft and affable.
    Why does the world report that Kate doth limp ?   245
    O sland'rous world !   Kate like the hazeltwig
    Is straight and slender, and as brown in hue
    As hazel-nuts, and sweeter than the kernels.
    O, let me see thee walk.   Thou dost not halt.
KATH. Go, fool, and whom thou keep'st command.   250
PET. Did ever Dian so become a grove
    As Kate this chamber with her princely gait ?
    O, be thou Dian, and let her be Kate ;
    And then let Kate be chaste, and Dian sportful !
KATH. Where did you study all this goodly speech ?   255
PET. It is extempore, from my mother wit.
KATH. A witty mother ! witless else her son.
PET. Am I not wise ?
KATH. Yes, keep you warm.
PET. Marry, so I mean, sweet Katherine, in thy bed.
    And therefore, setting all this chat aside,   260
    Thus in plain terms : your father hath consented
    That you shall be my wife ; your dowry 'greed on ;
    And will you, nill you, I will marry you.
    Now, Kate, I am a husband for your turn ;
    For, by this light, whereby I see thy beauty,   265
    Thy beauty that doth make me like thee well,
    Thou must be married to no man but me ;
    For I am he am born to tame you, Kate,
    And bring you from a wild Kate to a Kate
    Conformable as other household Kates.   270

              Re-enter BAPTISTA, GREMIO, *and* TRANIO.

Here comes your father.   Never make denial ;
I must and will have Katherine to my wife.
BAP. Now, Signior Petruchio, how speed you with my daughter ?
PET. How but well, sir ? how but well ?
It were impossible I should speed amiss.   275
BAP. Why, how now, daughter Katherine, in your dumps ?
KATH. Call you me daughter ?   Now I promise you
You have show'd a tender fatherly regard
To wish me wed to one half lunatic,
A mad-cap ruffian and a swearing Jack,   280
That thinks with oaths to face the matter out.
PET. Father, 'tis thus : yourself and all the world
That talk'd of her have talk'd amiss of her.
If she be curst, it is for policy,
For she's not froward, but modest as the dove ;   285
She is not hot, but temperate as the morn ;
For patience she will prove a second Grissel,
And Roman Lucrece for her chastity.
And, to conclude, we have 'greed so well together
That upon Sunday is the wedding-day.   290
KATH. I'll see thee hang'd on Sunday first.
GRE. Hark, Petruchio ; she says she'll see thee hang'd first.
TRA. Is this your speeding ?   Nay, then good-night our part !
PET. Be patient, gentlemen.   I choose her for myself ;
If she and I be pleas'd, what's that to you ?   295
'Tis bargain'd 'twixt us twain, being alone,
That she shall still be curst in company.
I tell you 'tis incredible to believe
How much she loves me—O, the kindest Kate !
She hung about my neck, and kiss on kiss   300
She vied so fast, protesting oath on oath,
That in a twink she won me to her love.
O, you are novices !   'Tis a world to see
How tame, when men and women are alone,
A meacock wretch can make the curstest shrew.   305
Give me thy hand, Kate ; I will unto Venice,
To buy apparel 'gainst the wedding-day.
Provide the feast, father, and bid the guests ;
I will be sure my Katherine shall be fine.
BAP. I know not what to say ; but give me your hands.   310
God send you joy, Petruchio !   'Tis a match.
GRE., TRA. Amen, say we ; we will be witnesses.
PET. Father, and wife, and gentlemen, adieu.
I will to Venice ; Sunday comes apace ;
We will have rings and things, and fine array ;   315
And kiss me, Kate ; we will be married a Sunday.
                    [exeunt PETRUCHIO and KATHERINA severally.
GRE. Was ever match clapp'd up so suddenly ?
BAP. Faith, gentlemen, now I play a merchant's part,
And venture madly on a desperate mart.
TRA. 'Twas a commodity lay fretting by you ;   320
'Twill bring you gain, or perish on the seas.
BAP. The gain I seek is quiet in the match.
GRE. No doubt but he hath got a quiet catch.

But now, Baptista, to your younger daughter :
Now is the day we long have looked for ;   325
I am your neighbour, and was suitor first.
TRA. And I am one that love Bianca more
Than words can witness or your thoughts can guess.
GRE. Youngling, thou canst not love so dear as I.
TRA. Greybeard, thy love doth freeze.
GRE.   But thine doth fry.   330
Skipper, stand back ; 'tis age that nourisheth.
TRA. But youth in ladies' eyes that flourisheth.
BAP. Content you, gentlemen ;   I will compound this strife.
'Tis deeds must win the prize, and he of both
That can assure my daughter greatest dower   335
Shall have my Bianca's love.
Say, Signior Gremio, what can you assure her ?
GRE. First, as you know, my house within the city
Is richly furnished with plate and gold,
Basins and ewers to lave her dainty hands ;   340
My hangings all of Tyrian tapestry ;
In ivory coffers I have stuff'd my crowns ;
In cypress chests my arras counterpoints,
Costly apparel, tents, and canopies,
Fine linen, Turkey cushions boss'd with pearl,   345
Valance of Venice gold in needle-work ;
Pewter and brass, and all things that belongs
To house or housekeeping.   Then at my farm
I have a hundred milch-kine to the pail,
Six score fat oxen standing in my stalls,   350
And all things answerable to this portion.
Myself am struck in years, I must confess ;
And if I die to-morrow this is hers,
If whilst I live she will be only mine.
TRA. That ' only ' came well in.   Sir, list to me :   355
I am my father's heir and only son ;
If I may have your daughter to my wife,
I'll leave her houses three or four as good
Within rich Pisa's walls as any one
Old Signior Gremio has in Padua ;   360
Besides two thousand ducats by the year
Of fruitful land, all which shall be her jointure.
What, have I pinch'd you, Signior Gremio ?
GRE. Two thousand ducats by the year of land !
[aside.]   My land amounts not to so much in all.—   365
That she shall have, besides an argosy
That now is lying in Marseilles road.
What, have I chok'd you with an argosy ?
TRA. Gremio, 'tis known my father hath no less
Than three great argosies, besides two galliasses,   370
And twelve tight galleys.   These I will assure her,
And twice as much whate'er thou off'rest next.
GRE. Nay, I have off'red all ;   I have no more ;
And she can have no more than all I have ;
If you like me, she shall have me and mine.   375

TRA. Why, then the maid is mine from all the world
  By your firm promise ; Gremio is out-vied.
BAP. I must confess your offer is the best ;
  And let your father make her the assurance,
  She is your own. Else, you must pardon me ;   380
  If you should die before him, where's her dower ?
TRA. That's but a cavil ; he is old, I young.
GRE. And may not young men die as well as old ?
BAP. Well, gentlemen,
  I am thus resolv'd : on Sunday next you know   385
  My daughter Katherine is to be married ;
  Now, on the Sunday following shall Bianca
  Be bride to you, if you make this assurance ;
  If not, to Signior Gremio.
  And so I take my leave, and thank you both.   390
GRE. Adieu, good neighbour.   *[exit* BAPTISTA.
            Now, I fear thee not.
  Sirrah young gamester, your father were a fool
  To give thee all, and in his waning age
  Set foot under thy table. Tut, a toy !
  An old Italian fox is not so kind, my boy.   *[exit.*
TRA. A vengeance on your crafty withered hide !
  Yet I have fac'd it with a card of ten.
  'Tis in my head to do my master good :
  I see no reason but suppos'd Lucentio
  Must get a father, call'd suppos'd Vincentio ;   400
  And that's a wonder—fathers commonly
  Do get their children ; but in this case of wooing
  A child shall get a sire, if I fail not of my cunning. *[exit.*

ACT THREE.

SCENE I. *Padua.* *Baptista's house.*

Enter LUCENTIO *as* CAMBIO, HORTENSIO *as* LICIO, *and* BIANCA.
LUC. Fiddler, forbear ; you grow too forward, sir.
  Have you so soon forgot the entertainment
  Her sister Katherine welcom'd you withal ?
HOR. But, wrangling pedant, this is
  The patroness of heavenly harmony.   5
  Then give me leave to have prerogative ;
  And when in music we have spent an hour,
  Your lecture shall have leisure for as much.
LUC. Preposterous ass, that never read so far
  To know the cause why music was ordain'd !   10
  Was it not to refresh the mind of man
  After his studies or his usual pain ?
  Then give me leave to read philosophy,
  And while I pause serve in your harmony.
HOR. Sirrah, I will not bear these braves of thine. 15
BIAN. Why, gentlemen, you do me double wrong
  To strive for that which resteth in my choice.
  I am no breeching scholar in the schools,

SCENE 3
*Interior. Baptista's
House. Day.*
LUCENTIO and
HORTENSIO enter
arguing.

BIANCA enters,
parting them.

I'll not be tied to hours nor 'pointed times,
But learn my lessons as I please myself.   20
And to cut off all strife : here sit we down ;
Take you your instrument, play you the whiles !
His lecture will be done ere you have tun'd.
HOR. You'll leave his lecture when I am in tune ?
LUC. That will be never—tune your instrument.   25
BIAN. Where left we last ?
LUC. Here, madam :
' Hic ibat Simois, hic est Sigeia tellus,
Hic steterat Priami regia celsa senis '.
BIAN. Construe them.   30
LUC. ' Hic ibat ' as I told you before—' Simois ' I am Lucentio—   HORTENSIO leaves.
' hic est ' son unto Vincentio of Pisa—' Sigeia tellus ' disguised
thus to get your love—' Hic steterat ' and that Lucentio that
comes a-wooing—' Priami ' is my man Tranio—' regia ' bearing
my port—' celsa senis ' that we might beguile the old pantaloon.
HOR. Madam, my instrument's in tune.   37   HORTENSIO returns.
BIAN. Let's hear.   O fie ! the treble jars.
LUC. Spit in the hole, man, and tune again.
BIAN. Now let me see if I can construe it : ' Hic ibat Simois ' I   HORTENSIO leaves and
know you not—' hic est Sigeia tellus ' I trust you not—' Hic   returns during this
steterat Priami ' take heed he hear us not—' regia ' presume   speech.
not—' celsa senis ' despair not.
HOR. Madam, 'tis now in tune.
LUC.   All but the bass.
HOR. The bass is right ; 'tis the base knave that jars.   45
[aside.]   How fiery and forward our pedant is !
Now, for my life, the knave doth court my love.
Pedascule, I'll watch you better yet.
BIAN. In time I may believe, yet I mistrust.
LUC. Mistrust it not—for sure, Æacides   50
Was Ajax, call'd so from his grandfather.
BIAN. I must believe my master ; else, I promise you,
I should be arguing still upon that doubt ;
But let it rest.   Now, Licio, to you.
Good master, take it not unkindly, pray,   55
That I have been thus pleasant with you both.
HOR. [to LUCENTIO.]   You may go walk and give me leave awhile ;
My lessons make no music in three parts.
LUC. Are you so formal, sir ?   Well, I must wait,
[aside.]   And watch withal ; for, but I be deceiv'd,   60
Our fine musician groweth amorous.
HOR. Madam, before you touch the instrument
To learn the order of my fingering,
I must begin with rudiments of art,
To teach you gamut in a briefer sort,   65
More pleasant, pithy, and effectual,
Than hath been taught by any of my trade;
And there it is in writing fairly drawn.
BIAN. Why, I am past my gamut long ago.
HOR. Yet read the gamut of Hortensio.   70
BIAN. [reads.]

    ' " Gamut " I am, the ground of all accord—
    " A re " to plead Horteniso's passion—
    " B mi " Bianca, take him for thy lord—
    " C fa ut " that loves with all affection—
    " D sol re " one clef, two notes have I—   75
    " E la mi " show pity or I die '.
Call you this gamut ?   Tut, I like it not !
Old fashions please me best ; I am not so nice
To change true rules for odd inventions.

             Enter a SERVANT.

SERV. Mistress, your father prays you leave your books   80
    And help to dress your sister's chamber up.
    You know to-morrow is the wedding-day.
BIAN. Farewell, sweet masters, both ; I must be gone.
               [*exeunt* BIANCA *and* SERVANT.
LUC. Faith, mistress, then I have no cause to stay.   [*exit.*
HOR. But I have cause to pry into this pedant ;
    Methinks he looks as though he were in love.
    Yet if thy thoughts, Bianca, be so humble
    To cast thy wand'ring eyes on every stale—
    Seize thee that list.   If once I find thee ranging,
    Hortensio will be quit with thee by changing.   [*exit.*

      SCENE II.   *Padua.   Before Baptista's house.*

Enter BAPTISTA, GREMIO, TRANIO *as* LUCENTIO, KATHERINA, BIANCA,
    LUCENTIO *as* CAMBIO, *and* ATTENDANTS.

BAP. [*to* TRANIO.]   Signior Lucentio, this is the 'pointed day
    That Katherine and Petruchio should be married,
    And yet we hear not of our son-in-law.
    What will be said ?   What mockery will it be
    To want the bridegroom when the priest attends   5
    To speak the ceremonial rites of marriage !
    What says Lucentio to this shame of ours ?
KATH. No shame but mine ;   I must, forsooth, be forc'd
    To give my hand, oppos'd against my heart,
    Unto a mad-brain rudesby, full of spleen,   10
    Who woo'd in haste and means to wed at leisure.
    I told you, I, he was a frantic fool,
    Hiding his bitter jests in blunt behaviour ;
    And, to be noted for a merry man,
    He'll woo a thousand, 'point the day of marriage,   15
    Make friends invited, and proclaim the banns ;
    Yet never means to wed where he hath woo'd.
    Now must the world point at poor Katherine,
    And say ' Lo, there is mad Petruchio's wife,
    If it would please him come and marry her ! '   20
TRA. Patience, good Katherine, and Baptista too.
    Upon my life, Petruchio means but well,
    Whatever fortune stays him from his word.
    Though he be blunt, I know him passing wise ;
    Though he be merry, yet withal he's honest.   25

SCENE 4
Exterior. Padua.
A Street. Day.
The characters
waiting impatiently.

KATH. Would Katherine had never seen him though !
          [*exit, weeping, followed by* BIANCA *and others.*
BAP. Go, girl, I cannot blame thee now to weep,
  For such an injury would vex a very saint ;
  Much more a shrew of thy impatient humour.

KATHERINA and the
others move up the
street.

Enter BIONDELLO.

BION. Master, master ! News, and such old news as you never
  heard of !   31
BAP. Is it new and old too ?   How may that be ?
BION. Why, is it not news to hear of Petruchio's coming ?
BAP. Is he come ?
BION. Why, no, sir.   35
BAP. What then ?
BION. He is coming.
BAP. When will he be here ?
BION. When he stands where I am and sees you there.
TRA. But, say, what to thine old news ?   40
BIAN. Why, Petruchio is coming—in a new hat and an old jerkin ;
  a pair of old breeches thrice turn'd ; a pair of boots that have
  been candle-cases, one buckled, another lac'd ; an old rusty
  sword ta'en out of the town armoury, with a broken hilt, and
  chapeless ; with two broken points ; his horse hipp'd, with an
  old motley saddle and stirrups of no kindred ; besides, possess'd
  with the glanders and like to mose in the chine, troubled with
  the lampass, infected with the fashions, full of windgalls, sped
  with spavins, rayed with the yellows, past cure of the fives, stark
  spoil'd with the staggers, begnawn with the bots, sway'd in the
  back and shoulder-shotten, near-legg'd before, and with a half-
  cheek'd bit, and a head-stall of sheep's leather which, being
  restrained to keep him from stumbling, hath been often burst,
  and now repaired with knots ; one girth six times piec'd, and a
  woman's crupper of velure, which hath two letters for her name
  fairly set down in studs, and here and there piec'd with pack-
  thread.
BAP. Who comes with him ?   60
BION. O, sir, his lackey, for all the world caparison'd like the horse—
  with a linen stock on one leg and a kersey boot-hose on the other,
  gart'red with a red and blue list ; an old hat, and the humour of
  forty fancies prick'd in't for a feather ; a monster, a very monster
  in apparel, and not like a Christian footboy or a gentleman's
  lackey.   67
TRA. 'Tis some odd humour pricks him to this fashion ;
  Yet oftentimes he goes but mean-appare'l'd.
BAP. I am glad he's come, howsoe'er he comes.   70
BION. Why, sir, he comes not.
BAP. Didst thou not say he comes ?
BION. Who ? that Petruchio came ?
BAP. Ay, that Petruchio came.
BION. No, sir ; I say his horse comes with him on his back.   76
BAP. Why, that's all one.
BION.   Nay, by Saint Jamy,
    I hold you a penny,
    A horse and a man   80

Is more than one,
And yet not many.

Enter PETRUCHIO *and* GRUMIO.

PET. Come, where be these gallants ?   Who's at home ?
BAP. You are welcome, sir.
PET.   And yet I come not well.
BAP. And yet you halt not.
TRA.   Not so well apparell'd   85
    As I wish you were.
PET. Were it better, I should rush in thus.
    But where is Kate ?   Where is my lovely bride ?
    How does my father ?   Gentles, methinks you frown ;
    And wherefore gaze this goodly company   90
    As if they saw some wondrous monument,
    Some comet or unusual prodigy ?
BAP. Why, sir, you know this is your wedding-day.
    First were we sad, fearing you would not come,
    Now sadder, that you come so unprovided.   95
    Fie, doff this habit, shame to your estate,
    An eye-sore to our solemn festival !
TRA. And tell us what occasion of import
    Hath all so long detain'd you from your wife,
    And sent you hither so unlike yourself ?   100
PET. Tedious it were to tell, and harsh to hear.
    Sufficeth I am come to keep my word,
    Though in some part enforced to digress,
    Which at more leisure I will so excuse
    As you shall well be satisfied withal.   105
    But where is Kate ?   I stay too long from her ;
    The morning wears, 'tis time we were at church.
TRA. See not your bride in these unreverent robes ;
    Go to my chamber, put on clothes of mine.
PET. Not I, believe me ; thus I'll visit her.   110
BAP. But thus, I trust, you will not marry her.
PET. Good sooth, even thus ; therefore ha' done with words ;
    To me she's married, not unto my clothes.
    Could I repair what she will wear in me
    As I can change these poor accoutrements,   115
    'Twere well for Kate and better for myself.
    But what a fool am I to chat with you,
    When I should bid good-morrow to my bride
    And seal the title with a lovely kiss !
                    [*exeunt* PETRUCHIO *and* GRUMIO.   PETRUCHIO sees
TRA. He hath some meaning in his mad attire.   120   KATHERINA, seizes
    We will persuade him, be it possible,   her and pulls her
    To put on better ere he go to church.   towards the church at
BAP. I'll after him and see the event of this.   the top of the street,
                [*exeunt* BAPTISTA, GREMIO, BIONDELLO, *and* ATTENDANTS.   followed by GRUMIO
TRA. But to her love concerneth us to add   and the others.
    Her father's liking ; which to bring to pass,   125   TRANIO, BIONDELLO
    As I before imparted to your worship,   and LUCENTIO
    I am to get a man—whate'er he be   remain.
    It skills not much ; we'll fit him to our turn—

And he shall be Vincentio of Pisa,
And make assurance here in Padua   130
Of greater sums than I have promised.
So shall you quietly enjoy your hope
And marry sweet Bianca with consent.
LUC. Were it not that my fellow schoolmaster
Doth watch Bianca's steps so narrowly,   135
'Twere good, methinks, to steal our marriage ;
Which once perform'd, let all the world say no,
I'll keep mine own despite of all the world.
TRA. That by degrees we mean to look into
And watch our vantage in this business ;   140
We'll over-reach the greybeard, Gremio,
The narrow-prying father, Minola,
The quaint musician, amorous Licio—
All for my master's sake, Lucentio.

                Re-enter GREMIO.

Signior Gremio, came you from the church ?   145
GRE. As willingly as e'er I came from school.
TRA. And is the bride and bridegroom coming home ?
GRE. A bridegroom, say you ?   'Tis a groom indeed,
A grumbling groom, and that the girl shall find.
TRA. Curster than she ?   Why, 'tis impossible.   150
GRE. Why, he's a devil, a devil, a very fiend.
TRA. Why, she's a devil, a devil, the devil's dam.
GRE. Tut, she's a lamb, a dove, a fool, to him !
I'll tell you, Sir Lucentio : when the priest
Should ask if Katherine should be his wife,   155
' Ay, by gogs-wouns ' quoth he, and swore so loud
That, all amaz'd, the priest let fall the book ;
And as he stoop'd again to take it up,
This mad-brain'd bridegroom took him such a cuff
That down fell priest and book, and book and priest. 160
' Now take them up ', quoth he ' if any list '.
TRA. What said the wench, when he rose again ?
GRE. Trembled and shook, for why he stamp'd and swore
As if the vicar meant to cozen him.
But after many ceremonies done   165
He calls for wine : ' A health ! ' quoth he, as if
He had been abroad, carousing to his mates
After a storm ; quaff'd off the muscadel,
And threw the sops all in the sexton's face,
Having no other reason   170
But that his beard grew thin and hungerly
And seem'd to ask him sops as he was drinking.
This done, he took the bride about the neck,
And kiss'd her lips with such a clamorous smack
That at the parting all the church did echo.   175
And I, seeing this, came thence for very shame ;
And after me, I know, the rout is coming.
Such a mad marriage never was before.
Hark, hark !   I hear the minstrels play.
                                    [*music plays.*

Enter PETRUCHIO, KATHERINA, BIANCA, BAPTISTA, HORTENSIO, GRUMIO,
and TRAIN.

PET. Gentlemen and friends, I thank you for your pains.   180
    I know you think to dine with me to-day,
    And have prepar'd great store of wedding cheer
    But so it is—my haste doth call me hence,
    And therefore here I mean to take my leave.
BAP. Is't possible you will away to-night?   185
PET. I must away to-day before night come.
    Make it no wonder; if you knew my business,
    You would entreat me rather go than stay.
    And, honest company, I thank you all
    That have beheld me give away myself   190
    To this most patient, sweet, and virtuous wife.
    Dine with my father, drink a health to me.
    For I must hence; and farewell to you all.
TRA. Let us entreat you stay till after dinner.
PET. It may not be.
GRE.   Let me entreat you.   195
PET. It cannot be.
KATH.   Let me entreat you.
PET. I am content.
KATH.   Are you content to stay?
PET. I am content you shall entreat me stay;
    But yet not stay, entreat me how you can.
KATH. Now, if you love me, stay.
PET.   Grumio, my horse.   200
GRU. Ay, sir, they be ready; the oats have eaten the horses.
KATH. Nay, then,
    Do what thou canst, I will not go to-day;
    No, nor to-morrow, not till I please myself.   205
    The door is open, sir; there lies your way;
    You may be jogging whiles your boots are green;
    For me, I'll not be gone till I please myself.
    'Tis like you'll prove a jolly surly groom
    That take it on you at the first so roundly.   210
PET. O Kate, content thee; prithee be not angry.
KATH. I will be angry; what hast thou to do?
    Father, be quiet; he shall stay my leisure.
GRE. Ay, marry, sir, now it begins to work.
KATH. Gentlemen, forward to the bridal dinner.   215
    I see a woman may be made a fool
    If she had not a spirit to resist.
PET. They shall go forward, Kate, at thy command.
    Obey the bride, you that attend on her;
    Go to the feast, revel and domineer,   220
    Carouse full measure to her maidenhead;
    Be mad and merry, or go hang yourselves.
    But for my bonny Kate, she must with me.
    Nay, look not big, nor stamp, nor stare, nor fret;
    I will be master of what is mine own—   225
    She is my goods, my chattels, she is my house,
    My household stuff, my field, my barn,

My horse, my ox, my ass, my any thing,
And here she stands ; touch her whoever dare ;
I'll bring mine action on the proudest he   230
That stops my way in Padua.   Grumio,
Draw forth thy weapon ; we are beset with thieves ;
Rescue thy mistress, if thou be a man.
Fear not, sweet wench ; they shall not touch thee, Kate ;
I'll buckler thee against a million.   235
           [*exeunt* PETRUCHIO, KATHERINA, *and* GRUMIO.
BAP. Nay, let them go, a couple of quiet ones.
GRE. Went they not quickly, I should die with laughing.
TRA. Of all mad matches, never was the like.
LUC. Mistress, what's your opinion of your sister ?
BIAN. That, being mad herself, she's madly mated.   240
GRE. I warrant him, Petruchio is Kated.
BAP. Neighbours and friends, though bride and bridegroom wants
    For to supply the places at the table,
    You know there wants no junkets at the feast.
    Lucentio, you shall supply the bridegroom's place ;   245
    And let Bianca take her sister's room.
TRA. Shall sweet Bianca practise how to bride it ?
BAP. She shall, Lucentio.   Come, gentlemen, let's go.   [*exeunt.*

ACT FOUR.

SCENE I.   *Petruchio's country house.*

Enter GRUMIO.

GRU. Fie, fie on all tired jades, on all mad masters, and all foul
ways !   Was ever man so beaten ?   Was ever man so ray'd ?
Was ever man so weary ?   I am sent before to make a fire, and
they are coming after to warm them.   Now were not I a little
pot and soon hot, my very lips might freeze to my teeth, my
tongue to the roof of my mouth, my heart in my belly, ere I
should come by a fire to thaw me.   But I with blowing the fire
shall warm myself ; for, considering the weather, a taller man
than I will take cold.   Holla, ho !   Curtis !   10

Enter CURTIS.

CURT. Who is that calls so coldly ?
GRU. A piece of ice.   If thou doubt it, thou mayst slide from my
  shoulder to my heel with no greater a run but my head and my
  neck.   A fire, good Curtis.
CURT. Is my master and his wife coming, Grumio ?   15
GRU. O, ay, Curtis, ay ; and therefore fire, fire ; cast on no water.
CURT. Is she so hot a shrew as she's reported ?
GRU. She was, good Curtis, before this frost ; but thou know'st
  winter tames man, woman, and beast ; for it hath tam'd my old
  master, and my new mistress, and myself, fellow Curtis.   22
CURT. Away, you three-inch fool !   I am no beast.

SCENE 5
*Interior. Petruchio's
House. Night.*

'Now were not . . . to
thaw me' omitted.

'If thou doubt . . .
and my neck'
omitted.

'but thou know'st
. . . I am no beast'
omitted.

GRU. Am I but three inches ? Why, thy horn is a foot, and so long am I at the least. But wilt thou make a fire, or shall I complain on thee to our mistress, whose hand—she being now at hand— thou shalt soon feel, to thy cold comfort, for being slow in thy hot office ?

'Am I but . . . at the least' omitted.
'whose hand . . . cold comfort' omitted.

CURT. I prithee, good Grumio, tell me how goes the world ?   30
GRU. A cold world, Curtis, in every office but thine ; and therefore fire. Do thy duty, and have thy duty, for my master and mistress are almost frozen to death.
CURT. There's fire ready ; and therefore, good Grumio, the news ?
GRU. Why, ' Jack boy ! ho, boy ! ' and as much news as thou wilt.
CURT. Come, you are so full of conycatching !   38
GRU. Why, therefore, fire ; for I have caught extreme cold. Where's the cook ? Is supper ready, the house trimm'd, rushes strew'd, cobwebs swept, the serving-men in their new fustian, their white stockings, and every officer his wedding-garment on ? Be the jacks fair within, the jills fair without, the carpets laid, and everything in order ?

'the serving-men . . . fair without' omitted.

CURT. All ready ; and therefore, I pray thee, news.   45
GRU. First know my horse is tired ; my master and mistress fall'n out.
CURT. How ?
GRU. Out of their saddles into the dirt ; and thereby hangs a tale.
CURT. Let's ha't, good Grumio.
GRU. Lend thine ear.
CURT. Here.
GRU. There.   [striking him.
CURT. This 'tis to feel a tale, not to hear a tale.   55
GRU. And therefore 'tis call'd a sensible tale ; and this cuff was but to knock at your ear and beseech list'ning. Now I begin : Imprimis, we came down a foul hill, my master riding behind my mistress—
CURT. Both of one horse ?   60
GRU. What's that to thee ?
CURT. Why, a horse.
GRU. Tell thou the tale. But hadst thou not cross'd me, thou shouldst have heard how her horse fell and she under her horse ; thou shouldst have heard in how miry a place, how she was bemoil'd, how he left her with the horse upon her, how he beat me because her horse stumbled, how she waded through the dirt to pluck him off me, how he swore, how she pray'd that never pray'd before, how I cried, how the horses ran away, how her bridle was burst, how I lost my crupper—with many things of worthy memory, which now shall die in oblivion, and thou return unexperienc'd to thy grave.   73
CURT. By this reck'ning he is more shrew than she.
GRU. Ay, and that thou and the proudest of you all shall find when he comes home. But what talk I of this ? Call forth Nathaniel, Joseph, Nicholas, Philip, Walter, Sugarsop, and the rest ; let their heads be sleekly comb'd, their blue coats brush'd and their garters of an indifferent knit ; let them curtsy with their left legs, and not presume to touch a hair of my master's horse-tail till they kiss their hands. Are they all ready ?   82

'let their heads . . . kiss their hands' omitted.

CURT. They are.
GRU. Call them forth.

CURT. Do you hear, ho ?   You must meet my master, to countenance
　my mistress.   86
GRU. Why, she hath a face of her own.
CURT. Who knows not that ?
GRU. Thou, it seems, that calls for company to countenance her.
CURT. I call them forth to credit her.
GRU. Why, she comes to borrow nothing of them.

Enter four or five SERVINGMEN.

NATH. Welcome home, Grumio !
PHIL. How now, Grumio !
JOS. What, Grumio !   95
NICH. Fellow Grumio !
NATH. How now, old lad !
GRU. Welcome, you !—how now, you !—what, you !—fellow, you !—
　and thus much for greeting.   Now, my spruce companions, is
　all ready, and all things neat ?   100
NATH. All things is ready.   How near is our master ?
GRU. E'en at hand, alighted by this ; and therefore be not—Cock's
　passion, silence !   I hear my master.

Enter PETRUCHIO *and* KATHERINA.

PET. Where be these knaves ?   What, no man at door
　To hold my stirrup nor to take my horse !   105
　Where is Nathaniel, Gregory, Philip ?
ALL SERV. Here, here, sir ;   here, sir.
PET. Here, sir ! here, sir ! here, sir ! here, sir !
　You logger-headed and unpolish'd grooms !
　What, no attendance ? no regard ? no duty ?   110
　Where is the foolish knave I sent before ?
GRU. Here, sir ; as foolish as I was before.
PET. You peasant swain ! you whoreson malt-horse drudge !
　Did I not bid thee meet me in the park
　And bring along these rascal knaves with thee ?   115
GRU. Nathaniel's coat, sir, was not fully made,
　And Gabriel's pumps were all unpink'd i' th' heel ;
　There was no link to colour Peter's hat,
　And Walter's dagger was not come from sheathing ;
　There were none fine but Adam, Ralph, and Gregory ;   120
　The rest were ragged, old, and beggarly ;
　Yet, as they are, here they come to meet you.
PET. Go, rascals, go and fetch my supper in.
　　　　　　　　　　　　　　　[exeunt some of the SERVINGMEN.
　[*Sings.*]   Where is the life that late I led ?
　　　　　　　Where are those—
　Sit down, Kate, and welcome.   Soud, soud, soud, soud !

Re-enter SERVANTS *with supper.*

Why, when, I say ?   Nay, good sweet Kate, be merry.
Off with my boots, you rogues ! you villains, when ?
[*Sings.*]   It was the friar of orders grey,
　　　　　As he forth walked on his way—
Out, you rogue ! you pluck my foot awry ;   130
Take that, and mend the plucking off the other.   [*strikes him.*

PETRUCHIO's next
speech is heard off
stage and under
GRUMIO's line.

For 'Soud, soud,
soud, soud !' read
'Food, food, food,
food !'

Sarah Badel as Katherina with, clockwise from top left, Grumio (David Kincaid), Nathaniel (Harry Webster), Gregory (Leslie Sarony), Nicholas (Derek Deadman), Peter (Denis Gilmore), Philip (Gil Morris) and Curtis (Angus Lennie)

67

Be merry, Kate.   Some water, here, what, ho !
                    Enter ONE *with water.*
Where's my spaniel Troilus ?   Sirrah, get you hence,   134
And bid my cousin Ferdinand come hither :   [*exit* SERVINGMAN.
One, Kate, that you must kiss and be acquainted with.
Where are my slippers ?   Shall I have some water ?
Come, Kate, and wash, and welcome heartily.
You whoreson villain ! will you let it fall ?   [*strikes him.*
KATH. Patience, I pray you ; 'twas a fault unwilling.   140
PET. A whoreson, beetle-headed, flap-ear'd knave !
Come, Kate, sit down ; I know you have a stomach.
Will you give thanks, sweet Kate, or else shall I ?
What's this ?   Mutton ?
I SERV.   Ay.
PET.   Who brought it ?
PETER.   I.
PET. 'Tis burnt ; and so is all the meat.   145
What dogs are these ?   Where is the rascal cook ?
How durst you villains bring it from the dresser
And serve it thus to me that love it not ?
There, take it to you, trenchers, cups, and all ;
                    [*throws the meat, etc., at them.*
You heedless joltheads and unmanner'd slaves !   150
What, do you grumble ?   I'll be with you straight.
                                        [*exeunt* SERVANTS.
KATH. I pray you, husband, be not so disquiet ;
The meat was well, if you were so contented.
PET. I tell thee, Kate, 'twas burnt and dried away,
And I expressly am forbid to touch it ;   155
For it engenders choler, planteth anger :
And better 'twere that both of us did fast,
Since, of ourselves, ourselves are choleric,
Than feed it with such over-roasted flesh.
Be patient ; to-morrow 't shall be mended.   160
And for this night we'll fast for company.
Come, I will bring thee to thy bridal chamber.   [*exeunt.*

                Re-enter SERVANTS *severally.*

NATH. Peter, didst ever see the like ?
PETER. He kills her in her own humour.
                    Re-enter CURTIS.
GRU. Where is he ?   165
CURT. In her chamber.   Making a sermon of continency to her,
And rails, and swears, and rates, that she, poor soul,
Knows not which way to stand, to look, to speak,
And sits as one new risen from a dream.   170
Away, away ! for he is coming hither.   [*exeunt.*
                Re-enter PETRUCHIO.
PET. Thus have I politicly begun my reign,
And 'tis my hope to end successfully.
My falcon now is sharp and passing empty.
And till she stoop she must not be full-gorg'd,   175

For then she never looks upon her lure.
Another way I have to man my haggard,
To make her come, and know her keeper's call,
That is, to watch her, as we watch these kites
That bate and beat, and will not be obedient.   180
She eat no meat to-day, nor none shall eat ;
Last night she slept not, nor to-night she shall not ;
As with the meat, some undeserved fault
I'll find about the making of the bed ;
And here I'll fling the pillow, there the bolster,   185
This way the coverlet, another way the sheets ;
Ay, and amid this hurly I intend
That all is done in reverend care of her—
And, in conclusion, she shall watch all night ;
And if she chance to nod I'll rail and brawl   190
And with the clamour keep her still awake.
This is a way to kill a wife with kindness,
And thus I'll curb her mad and headstrong humour.
He that knows better how to tame a shrew,
Now let him speak ; 'tis charity to show.   [exit.

SCENE II. *Padua. Before Baptista's house.*

Enter TRANIO *as* LUCENTIO, *and* HORTENSIO *as* LICIO.

TRA. Is't possible, friend Licio, that Mistress Bianca
Doth fancy any other but Lucentio ?
I tell you, sir, she bears me fair in hand.
HOR. Sir, to satisfy you in what I have said,
Stand by and mark the manner of his teaching. [*they stand aside.*

Enter BIANCA *and* LUCENTIO *as* CAMBIO.

LUC. Now, mistress profit you in what you read ?
BIAN. What, master, read you ? First resolve me that
LUC. I read that I profess, ' The Art to Love '.
BIAN. And may you prove, sir, master of your art !
LUC. While you, sweet dear, prove mistress of my heart.   10
[*they retire.*
HOR. Quick proceeders, marry ! Now tell me, I pray,
You that durst swear that your Mistress Bianca
Lov'd none in the world so well as Lucentio.
TRA. O despiteful love ! unconstant womankind !
I tell thee, Licio, this is wonderful.   15
HOR. Mistake no more ; I am not Licio.
Nor a musician as I seem to be ;
But one that scorn to live in this disguise
For such a one as leaves a gentleman
And makes a god of such a cullion.   20
Know, sir, that I am call'd Hortensio.
TRA. Signior Hortensio, I have often heard
Of your entire affection to Bianca ;
And since mine eyes are witness of her lightness,
I will with you, if you be so contented,   25
Forswear Bianca and her love for ever.
HOR. See, how they kiss and court ! Signior Lucentio

SCENE 6
Exterior. Padua.
A Street. Day.

69

Here is my hand, and here I firmly vow
Never to woo her more, but do forswear her,
As one unworthy all the former favours   30
That I have fondly flatter'd her withal.
TRA. And here I take the like unfeigned oath,
Never to marry with her though she would entreat;
Fie on her !   See how beastly she doth court him !
HOR. Would all the world but he had quite forsworn !   35
For me, that I may surely keep mine oath,
I will be married to a wealthy widow
Ere three days pass, which hath as long lov'd me
As I have lov'd this proud disdainful haggard.
And so farewell, Signior Lucentio.   40
Kindness in women, not their beauteous looks,
Shall win my love ; and so I take my leave,
In resolution as I swore before.   [exit.
TRA. Mistress Bianca, bless you with such grace
As 'longeth to a lover's blessed case !   45
Nay, I have ta'en you napping, gentle love,
And have forsworn you with Hortensio.
BIAN. Tranio, you jest ; but have you both forsworn me ?
TRA. Mistress, we have.
LUC.   Then we are rid of Licio.
TRA. I' faith, he'll have a lusty widow now,   50
That shall be woo'd and wedded in a day.
BIAN. God give him joy !
TRA. Ay, and he'll tame her.
BIAN.   He says so, Tranio.
TRA. Faith, he is gone unto the taming-school.
BIAN. The taming-school !   What, is there such a place ?   55
TRA. Ay, mistress ; and Petruchio is the master,
That teacheth tricks eleven and twenty long,
To tame a shrew and charm her chattering tongue.

Enter BIONDELLO.

BION. O master, master, I have watch'd so long
That I am dog-weary ; but at last I spied   60
An ancient angel coming down the hill
Will serve the turn.
TRA.   What is he, Biondello ?
BION. Master, a mercatante or a pedant,
I know not what ; but formal in apparel,
In gait and countenance surely like a father.   65
LUC. And what of him, Tranio ?
TRA. If he be credulous and trust my tale,
I'll make him glad to seem Vincentio,
And give assurance to Baptista Minola
As if he were the right Vincentio.   70
Take in your love, and then let me alone.
                    [*exeunt* LUCENTIO *and* BIANCA.

Enter a PEDANT.

PED. God save you, sir !
TRA. And you, sir ; you are welcome.

Travel you far on, or are you at the farthest?
PED. Sir, at the farthest for a week or two;
   But then up farther, and as far as Rome   75
   And so to Tripoli, if God lend me life.
TRA. What countryman, I pray?
PED.   Of Mantua.
TRA. Of Mantua, sir? Marry, God forbid,
   And come to Padua, careless of your life!
PED. My life, sir! How, I pray? For that goes hard.   80
TRA. 'Tis death for any one in Mantua
   To come to Padua. Know you not the cause?
   Your ships are stay'd at Venice; and the Duke,
   For private quarrel 'twixt your Duke and him,
   Hath publish'd and proclaim'd it openly.   85
   'Tis marvel—but that you are but newly come,
   You might have heard it else proclaim'd about.
PED. Alas, sir, it is worse for me than so!
   For I have bills for money by exchange
   From Florence, and must here deliver them.   90
TRA. Well, sir, to do you courtesy,
   This will I do, and this I will advise you—
   First, tell me, have you ever been at Pisa?
PED. Ay, sir, in Pisa have I often been,
   Pisa renowned for grave citizens.   95
TRA. Among them know you one Vincentio?
PED. I know him not, but I have heard of him,
   A merchant of incomparable wealth.
TRA. He is my father, sir; and, sooth to say,
   In count'nance somewhat doth resemble you.   100
BION. [aside.] As much as an apple doth an oyster, and all one.
TRA. To save your life in this extremity,
   This favour will I do you for his sake;
   And think it not the worst of all your fortunes
   That you are like to Sir Vincentio.   105
   His name and credit shall you undertake,
   And in my house you shall be friendly lodg'd;
   Look that you take upon you as you should.
   You understand me, sir. So shall you stay
   Till you have done your business in the city.   110
   If this be court'sy, sir, accept of it.
PED. O, sir, I do; and will repute you ever
   The patron of my life and liberty.
TRA. Then go with me to make the matter good.
   This, by the way, I let you understand: 115
   My father is here look'd for every day
   To pass assurance of a dow'r in marriage
   'Twixt me and one Baptista's daughter here.
   In all these circumstances I'll instruct you.
   Go with me to clothe you as becomes you.   [exeunt.

SCENE III. *Petruchio's house.*

Enter KATHERINA *and* GRUMIO.

GRU. No, no, forsooth; I dare not for my life.

SCENE 7
*Interior. Petruchio's
House. Day.*

71

KATH. The more my wrong, the more his spite appears.
    What, did he marry me to famish me ?
    Beggars that come unto my father's door
    Upon entreaty have a present alms ;   5
    If not, elsewhere they meet with charity ;
    But I, who never knew how to entreat,
    Nor never needed that I should entreat,
    Am starv'd for meat, giddy for lack of sleep ;
    With oaths kept waking, and with brawling fed ;   10
    And that which spites me more than all these wants—
    He does it under name of perfect love ;
    As who should say, if I should sleep or eat,
    'Twere deadly sickness or else present death.
    I prithee go and get me some repast ;   15
    I care not what, so it be wholesome food.
GRU. What say you to a neat's foot ?
KATH. 'Tis passing good ; I prithee let me have it.
GRU. I fear it is too choleric a meat.
    How say you to a fat tripe finely broil'd ?   20
KATH. I like it well ; good Grumio, fetch it me.
GRU. I cannot tell ; I fear 'tis choleric.
    What say you to a piece of beef and mustard ?
KATH. A dish that I do love to feed upon.
GRU. Ay, but the mustard is too hot a little.   25
KATH. Why then the beef, and let the mustard rest.
GRU. Nay, then I will not ; you shall have the mustard,
    Or else you get no beef of Grumio.
KATH. Then both, or one, or anything thou wilt.
GRU. Why then the mustard without the beef.   30
KATH. Go, get thee gone, thou false deluding slave,   *[beats him.*
    That feed'st me with the very name of meat.
    Sorrow on thee and all the pack of you
    That triumph thus upon my misery !
    Go, get thee gone, I say.   35

        Enter PETRUCHIO, *and* HORTENSIO *with meat.*

PET. How fares my Kate ? What, sweeting, all amort ?
HOR. Mistress, what cheer ?
KATH.   Faith, as cold as can be.
PET. Pluck up thy spirits, look cheerfully upon me.
    Here, love, thou seest how diligent I am,
    To dress thy meat myself, and bring it thee.   40
    I am sure, sweet Kate, this kindness merits thanks.
    What, not a word ? Nay, then thou lov'st it not,
    And all my pains is sorted to no proof.
    Here, take away this dish.
KATH.   I pray you, let it stand.
PET. The poorest service is repaid with thanks ;   45
    And so shall mine, before you touch the meat.
KATH. I thank you, sir.
HOR. Signior Petruchio, fie ! you are to blame.
    Come, Mistress Kate, I'll bear you company.
PET. [*aside.*] Eat it up all, Hortensio, if thou lovest me.   50
    Much good do it unto thy gentle heart !

Kate, eat apace. And now, my honey love,
Will we return unto thy father's house
And revel it as bravely as the best,
With silken coats and caps, and golden rings,   55
With ruffs and cuffs and farthingales and things,
With scarfs and fans and double change of brav'ry.
With amber bracelets, beads, and all this knav'ry.
What, hast thou din'd? The tailor stays thy leisure,
To deck thy body with his ruffling treasure.   60

CURTIS enters and
whispers to
PETRUCHIO.

Enter TAILOR.

Come, tailor, let us see these ornaments;
Lay forth the gown.

Enter HABERDASHER.

What news with you, sir?
HAB. Here is the cap your worship did bespeak.
PET. Why, this was moulded on a porringer;
A velvet dish. Fie, fie! 'tis lewd and filthy;   65
Why, 'tis a cockle or a walnut-shell,
A knack, a toy, a trick, a baby's cap.
Away with it. Come, let me have a bigger.
KATH. I'll have no bigger; this doth fit the time,
And gentlewomen wear such caps as these.   70
PET. When you are gentle, you shall have one too,
And not till then.
HOR. [*aside.*] That will not be in haste.
KATH. Why, sir, I trust I may have leave to speak;
And speak I will. I am no child, no babe.
Your betters have endur'd me say my mind,   75
And if you cannot, best you stop your ears.
My tongue will tell the anger of my heart,
Or else my heart, concealing it, will break;
And rather than it shall, I will be free
Even to the uttermost, as I please, in words.   80
PET. Why, thou say'st true; it is a paltry cap,
A custard-coffin, a bauble, a silken pie;
I love thee well in that thou lik'st it not.
KATH. Love me or love me not, I like the cap;
And it I will have, or I will have none.   [*exit* HABERDASHER.
PET. Thy gown? Why, ay. Come, tailor, let us see't.
O mercy, God! what masquing stuff is here?
What's this? A sleeve? 'Tis like a demi-cannon.
What, up and down, carv'd like an appletart?
Here's snip and nip and cut and slish and slash,   90
Like to a censer in a barber's shop.
Why, what a devil's name, tailor, call'st thou this?
HOR. [*aside.*] I see she's like to have neither cap nor gown.
TAI. You bid me make it orderly and well,
According to the fashion and the time.   95
PET. Marry, and did; but if you be rememb'red,
I did not bid you mar it to the time.
Go, hop me over every kennel home,
For you shall hop without my custom, sir.
I'll none of it; hence! make your best of it.   100

Katherina (Sarah Badel) and Petruchio (John Cleese) with the Haberdasher (David Kinsey) and, in the background, Hortensio (Jonathan Cecil)

KATH. I never saw a better fashion'd gown,
More quaint, more pleasing, nor more commendable ;
Belike you mean to make a puppet of me.
PET. Why, true ; he means to make a puppet of thee.
TAI. She says your worship means to make a puppet of her.   105
PET. O monstrous arrogance ! Thou liest, thou thread, thou thimble,
Thou yard, three-quarters, half-yard, quarter, nail,
Thou flea, thou nit, thou winter-cricket thou—
Brav'd in mine own house with a skein of thread !   110
Away, thou rag, thou quantity, thou remnant ;
Or I shall so bemete thee with thy yard
As thou shalt think on prating whilst thou liv'st !
I tell thee, I, that thou hast marr'd her gown.
TAI. Your worship is deceiv'd ; the gown is made   115
Just as my master had direction.
Grumio gave order how it should be done.
GRU. I gave him no order ; I gave him the stuff.
TAI. But how did you desire it should be made ?
GRU. Marry, sir, with needle and thread.   120
TAI. But did you not request to have it cut ?
GRU. Thou hast fac'd many things.
TAI. I have.
GRU. Face not me. Thou hast brav'd many men ; brave not me.
I will neither be fac'd nor brav'd. I say unto thee, I bid thy
master cut out the gown ; but I did not bid him cut it to pieces.
Ergo, thou liest.   127
TAI. Why, here is the note of the fashion to testify.
PET. Read it.
GRU. The note lies in's throat, if he say I said so.   130
TAI. [reads.] ' Imprimis, a loose-bodied gown '—
GRU. Master, if ever I said loose-bodied gown, sew me in the skirts
of it and beat me to death with a bottom of brown bread ; I
said a gown.
PET. Proceed.   135
TAI. [reads.] ' With a small compass'd cape '—
GRU. I confess the cape.
TAI. [reads.] ' With a trunk sleeve '—
GRU. I confess two sleeves.
TAI. [reads.] ' The sleeves curiously cut '.   140
PET. Ay, there's the villainy.
GRU. Error i' th' bill, sir ; error i' th' bill ! I commanded the sleeves
should be cut out, and sew'd up again ; and that I'll prove upon
thee, though thy little finger be armed in a thimble.
TAI. This is true that I say ; an I had thee in place where, thou
shouldst know it.
GRU. I am for thee straight ; take thou the bill, give me thy mete-
yard, and spare not me.
HOR. God-a-mercy, Grumio ! Then he shall have no odds.   150
PET. Well, sir, in brief, the gown is not for me.
GRU. You are i' th' right, sir ; 'tis for my mistress.
PET. Go, take it up unto thy master's use.
GRU. Villain, not for thy life ! Take up my mistress' gown for thy
master's use !   155
PET. Why, sir, what's your conceit in that ?

GRU. O, sir, the conceit is deeper than you think for.
　　Take up my mistress' gown to his master's use !
　　O fie, fie, fie !
PET. [*aside.*] Hortensio, say thou wilt see the tailor paid.——   160
　　Go take it hence ; be gone, and say no more.
HOR. Tailor, I'll pay thee for thy gown to-morrow ;
　　Take no unkindness of his hasty words.
　　Away, I say ; commend me to thy master.   [*exit* TAILOR.
PET. Well, come, my Kate ; we will unto your father's   165
　　Even in these honest mean habiliments ;
　　Our purses shall be proud, our garments poor ;
　　For 'tis the mind that makes the body rich ;
　　And as the sun breaks through the darkest clouds,
　　So honour peereth in the meanest habit.   170
　　What, is the jay more precious than the lark
　　Because his feathers are more beautiful ?
　　Or is the adder better than the eel
　　Because his painted skin contents the eye ?
　　O no, good Kate ; neither art thou the worse   175
　　For this poor furniture and mean array.
　　If thou account'st it shame, lay it on me ;
　　And therefore frolic ; we will hence forthwith
　　To feast and sport us at thy father's house.
　　Go call my men, and let us straight to him ;   180
　　And bring our horses unto Long-lane end ;
　　There will we mount, and thither walk on foot.
　　Let's see ; I think 'tis now some seven o'clock,
　　And well we may come there by dinner-time.
KATH. I dare assure you, sir, 'tis almost two,   185
　　And 'twill be supper-time ere you come there.
PET. It shall be seven ere I go to horse.
　　Look what I speak, or do, or think to do,
　　You are still crossing it. Sirs, let't alone ;
　　I will not go to-day ; and ere I do,   190
　　It shall be what o'clock I say it is.
HOR. Why, so this gallant will command the sun.   [*exeunt.*

SCENE IV. Padua. Before Baptista's house.

Enter TRANIO *as* LUCENTIO, *and the* PEDANT *dressed like* VINCENTIO.

SCENE 8
*Exterior. Padua.
A Street. Day.*

TRA. Sir, this is the house ; please it you that I call ?
PED. Ay, what else ? And, but I be deceived,
　　Signior Baptista may remember me
　　Near twenty years ago in Genoa,
　　Where we were lodgers at the Pegasus.
TRA. 'Tis well ; and hold your own, in any case,   5
　　With such austerity as longeth to a father.

Enter BIONDELLO.

PED. I warrant you. But, sir, here comes your boy ;
　　'Twere good he were school'd.
TRA. Fear you not him. Sirrah Biondello,   10
　　Now do your duty throughly, I advise you.
　　Imagine 'twere the right Vincentio.

BION. Tut, fear not me.
TRA. But hast thou done thy errand to Baptista?
BION. I told him that your father was at Venice,   15
  And that you look'd for him this day in Padua.
TRA. Th'art a tall fellow; hold thee that to drink.
  Here comes Baptista.   Set your countenance, sir.

    Enter BAPTISTA, *and* LUCENTIO *as* CAMBIO.

  Signior Baptista, you are happily met.
  [*to the* PEDANT.]   Sir, this is the gentleman I told you of;   20
  I pray you stand good father to me now;
  Give me Bianca for my patrimony.
PED. Soft, son!
  Sir, by your leave: having come to Padua
  To gather in some debts, my son Lucentio   25
  Made me acquainted with a weighty cause
  Of love between your daughter and himself;
  And—for the good report I hear of you,
  And for the love he beareth to your daughter,
  And she to him—to stay him not too long,   30
  I am content, in a good father's care,
  To have him match'd; and, if you please to like
  No worse than I, upon some agreement
  Me shall you find ready and willing
  With one consent to have her so bestow'd;   35
  For curious I cannot be with you,
  Signior Baptista, of whom I hear so well.
BAP. Sir, pardon me in what I have to say.
  Your plainness and your shortness please me well.
  Right true it is your son Lucentio here   40
  Doth love my daughter, and she loveth him,
  Or both dissemble deeply their affections;
  And therefore, if you say no more than this,
  That like a father you will deal with him,
  And pass my daughter a sufficient dower,   45
  The match is made, and all is done—
  Your son shall have my daughter with consent.
TRA. I thank you, sir.   Where then do you know best
  We be affied, and such assurance ta'en
  As shall with either part's agreement stand?   50
BAP. Not in my house, Lucentio, for you know
  Pitchers have ears, and I have many servants;
  Besides, old Gremio is heark'ning still,
  And happily we might be interrupted.
TRA. Then at my lodging, an it like you.   55
  There doth my father lie; and there this night
  We'll pass the business privately and well.
  Send for your daughter by your servant here;
  My boy shall fetch the scrivener presently.
  The worst is this, that at so slender warning   60
  You are like to have a thin and slender pittance.
BAP. It likes me well.   Cambio, hie you home,
  And bid Bianca make her ready straight;
  And, if you will, tell what hath happened—

Lucentio's father is arriv'd in Padua,   65
And how she's like to be Lucentio's wife.   [*exit* LUCENTIO.
BION. I pray the gods she may, with all my heart.
TRA. Dally not with the gods, but get thee gone.   [*exit* BIONDELLO.
Signior Baptista, shall I lead the way ?
Welcome !   One mess is like to be your cheer ;   70
Come, sir ; we will better it in Pisa.
BAP. I follow you.   [*exeunt.*

      Re-enter LUCENTIO *as* CAMBIO, *and* BIONDELLO.

BION. Cambio.
LUC. What say'st thou, Biondello ?
BION. You saw my master wink and laugh upon you ?   75
LUC. Biondello, what of that ?
BION. Faith, nothing ; but has left me here behind to expound the
meaning or moral of his signs and tokens.
LUC. I pray thee moralize them.
BION. Then thus : Baptista is safe, talking with the deceiving father
of a deceitful son.   81
LUC. And what of him ?
BION. His daughter is to be brought by you to the supper.
LUC. And then ?
BION. The old priest at Saint Luke's church is at your command at
all hours.
LUC. And what of all this ?
BION. I cannot tell, except they are busied about a counterfeit
assurance. Take your assurance of her, cum privilegio ad
imprimendum solum ; to th' church take the priest, clerk, and
some sufficient honest witnesses.   91
If this be not that you look for, I have no more to say,
But bid Bianca farewell for ever and a day.
LUC. Hear'st thou, Biondello ?   94
BION. I cannot tarry.   I knew a wench married in an afternoon as
she went to the garden for parsley to stuff a rabbit ; and so may
you, sir ; and so adieu, sir.   My master hath appointed me to
go to Saint Luke's to bid the priest be ready to come against you
come with your appendix.   [*exit.*
LUC. I may and will, if she be so contented.   100
She will be pleas'd ; then wherefore should I doubt ?
Hap what hap may, I'll roundly go about her ;
It shall go hard if Cambio go without her.   [*exit.*

              SCENE V.   *A public road.*

    Enter PETRUCHIO, KATHERINA, HORTENSIO, *and* SERVANTS.

PET. Come on, a God's name ; once more toward our father's.
Good Lord, how bright and goodly shines the moon !
KATH. The moon ?   The sun !   It is not moonlight now.
PET. I say it is the moon that shines so bright.
KATH. I know it is the sun that shines so bright.   5
PET. Now by my mother's son, and that's myself
It shall be moon, or star, or what I list,
Or ere I journey to your father's house.
Go on and fetch our horses back again.

LUCENTIO leaves,
passing GREMIO
entering. Scene ends
on GREMIO alone.

SCENE 9
*Exterior. Road to
Padua. Day.*

Evermore cross'd and cross'd ; nothing but cross'd !   10
HOR. Say as he says, or we shall never go.
KATH. Forward, I pray, since we have come so far,
   And be it moon, or sun, or what you please ;
   And if you please to call it a rush-candle,
   Henceforth I vow it shall be so for me.   15
PET. I say it is the moon.
KATH.   I know it is the moon.
PET. Nay, then you lie ; it is the blessed sun.
KATH. Then, God be bless'd, it is the blessed sun ;
   But sun it is not, when you say it is not ;
   And the moon changes even as your mind.   20
   What you will have it nam'd, even that it is,
   And so it shall be so for Katherine.
HOR. Petruchio, go thy ways, the field is won.
PET. Well, forward, forward ! thus the bowl should run,
   And not unluckily against the bias.   25
   But, soft ! Company is coming here.

                  Enter VINCENTIO.

[*to* VINCENTIO.]   Good-morrow, gentle mistress ; where away ?—
   Tell me, sweet Kate, and tell me truly too,
   Hast thou beheld a fresher gentlewoman ?
   Such war of white and red within her cheeks !   30
   What stars do spangle heaven with such beauty
   As those two eyes become that heavenly face ?
   Fair lovely maid, once more good day to thee.
   Sweet Kate, embrace her for her beauty's sake.
HOR. 'A will make the man mad, to make a woman of him.   35
KATH. Young budding virgin, fair and fresh and sweet,
   Whither away, or where is thy abode ?
   Happy the parents of so fair a child ;
   Happier the man whom favourable stars
   Allots thee for his lovely bed-fellow.   40
PET. Why, how now, Kate, I hope thou art not mad!
   This is a man, old, wrinkled, faded, withered,
   And not a maiden, as thou sayst he is.
KATH. Pardon, old father, my mistaking eyes,
   That have been so bedazzled with the sun   45
   That everything I look on seemeth green ;
   Now I perceive thou art a reverend father.
   Pardon, I pray thee, for my mad mistaking.
PET. Do, good old grandsire, and withal make known
   Which way thou travellest—if along with us,   50
   We shall be joyful of thy company.
VIN. Fair sir, and you my merry mistress,
   That with your strange encounter much amaz'd me,
   My name is call'd Vincentio, my dwelling Pisa,
   And bound I am to Padua, there to visit   55
   A son of mine, which long I have not seen.
PET. What is his name ?
VIN.   Lucentio, gentle sir.
PET. Happily met ; the happier for thy son.
   And now by law, as well as reverend age,

I may entitle thee my loving father :   60
The sister to my wife, this gentlewoman,
Thy son by this hath married.   Wonder not,
Nor be not grieved—she is of good esteem,
Her dowry wealthy, and of worthy birth ;
Beside, so qualified as may beseem   65
The spouse of any noble gentleman.
Let me embrace with old Vincentio ;
And wander we to see thy honest son,
Who will of thy arrival be full joyous.

VIN. But is this true ; or is it else your pleasure,   70
Like pleasant travellers, to break a jest
Upon the company you overtake ?

HOR. I do assure thee, father, so it is.

PET. Come, go along, and see the truth hereof ;
For our first merriment hath made thee jealous.   75
                              [*exeunt all but* HORTENSIO.

HOR. Well, Petruchio, this has put me in heart.
Have to my widow ; and if she be froward,
Then hast thou taught Hortensio to be untoward.   [*exit.*

ACT FIVE.

SCENE 10
Exterior. Padua.
A Street. Day.

SCENE I. *Padua.   Before Lucentio's house.*

Enter BIONDELLO, LUCENTIO, *and* BIANCA ; GREMIO *is out before.*

BION. Softly and swiftly, sir, for the priest is ready.

LUC. I fly, Biondello ; but they may chance to need thee at home,
therefore leave us.

BION. Nay, faith, I'll see the church a your back, and then come
back to my master's as soon as I can.   5
              [*exeunt* LUCENTIO, BIANCA, *and* BIONDELLO.

GRE. I marvel Cambio comes not all this while.

GREMIO discovered, waiting.

Enter PETRUCHIO, KATHERINA, VINCENTIO, GRUMIO, *and* ATTENDANTS.

PET. Sir, here's the door ; this is Lucentio's house ;
My father's bears more toward the market-place ;
Thither must I, and here I leave you, sir.

VIN. You shall not choose but drink before you go ;   10
I think I shall command your welcome here,
And by all likelihood some cheer is toward.   [*knocks.*

GRE. They're busy within ; you were best knock louder.

PEDANT *looks out of the window.*

PED. What's he that knocks as he would beat down the gate ?

VIN. Is Signior Lucentio within, sir ?

PED. He's within, sir, but not to be spoken withal.

VIN. What if a man bring him a hundred pound or two to make
merry withal ?

PED. Keep your hundred pounds to yourself ; he shall need none so
long as I live.   21

PET. Nay, I told you your son was well beloved in Padua.   Do you
hear, sir ?   To leave frivolous circumstances, I pray you tell

Signior Lucentio that his father is come from Pisa, and is here
at the door to speak with him.

PED. Thou liest : his father is come from Padua, and here looking
out at the window.   27

VIN. Art thou his father ?

PED. Ay, sir ; so his mother says, if I may believe her.

PET. [to VINCENTIO.] Why, how now, gentleman ! Why, this is
flat knavery to take upon you another man's name.   31

PED. Lay hands on the villain ; I believe 'a means to cozen somebody
in this city under my countenance.

Re-enter BIONDELLO.

BION. I have seen them in the church together. God send 'em
good shipping ! But who is here ? Mine old master, Vincentio !
Now we are undone and brought to nothing.   37

VIN. [*seeing* BIONDELLO.] Come hither, crack-hemp.

BION. I hope I may choose, sir.

VIN. Come hither, you rogue. What, have you forgot me ?

BION. Forgot you ! No, sir. I could not forget you, for I never saw
you before in all my life.

VIN. What, you notorious villain, didst thou never see thy master's
father, Vincentio ?   45

BION. What, my old worshipful old master ? Yes, marry, sir ; see
where he looks out of the window.

VIN. Is't so, indeed ?   [*he beats* BIONDELLO.

BION. Help, help, help ! Here's a madman will murder me.   [*exit.*

PED. Help, son ! help, Signior Baptista !   [*exit from above.*

PET. Prithee, Kate, let's stand aside and see the end of this controversy.
                                                   [*they stand aside.*

Re-enter PEDANT *below ;* BAPTISTA, TRANIO, *and* SERVANTS.

TRA. Sir, what are you that offer to beat my servant ?

VIN. What am I, sir ? Nay, what are you, sir ? O immortal gods !
O fine villain ! A silken doublet, a velvet hose, a scarlet cloak,
and a copatain hat ! O, I am undone ! I am undone ! While I
play the good husband at home, my son and my servant spend
all at the university.

TRA. How now ! what's the matter ?   60

BAP. What, is the man lunatic ?

TRA. Sir, you seem a sober ancient gentleman by your habit, but
your words show you a madman. Why, sir, what 'cerns it you
if I wear pearl and gold ? I thank my good father, I am able to
maintain it.

VIN. Thy father ! O villain ! he is a sailmaker in Bergamo.

BAP. You mistake, sir ; you mistake, sir. Pray, what do you think
is his name ?   69

VIN. His name ! As if I knew not his name ! I have brought him
up ever since he was three years old, and his name is Tranio.

PED. Away, away, mad ass ! His name is Lucentio ; and he is mine
only son, and heir to the lands of me, Signior Vincentio.   75

VIN. Lucentio ! O, he hath murd'red his master ! Lay hold on
him, I charge you, in the Duke's name. O, my son, my son !
Tell me, thou villain, where is my son, Lucentio ?   80

TRA. Call forth an officer.

Enter ONE *with an* OFFICER.   *Enter* OFFICER *alone.*

Carry this mad knave to the gaol. Father Baptista, I charge you
  see that he be forthcoming.
VIN. Carry me to the gaol !
GRE. Stay, Officer ; he shall not go to prison.
BAP. Talk not, Signior Gremio ; I say he shall go to prison.   86
GRE. Take heed, Signior Baptista, lest you be cony-catch'd in this
  business ; I dare swear this is the right Vincentio.
PED. Swear if thou dar'st.   90
GRE. Nay, I dare not swear it.
TRA. Then thou wert best say that I am not Lucentio.
GRE. Yes, I know thee to be Signior Lucentio.
BAP. Away with the dotard ; to the gaol with him !
VIN. Thus strangers may be hal'd and abus'd. O monstrous villain !

Re-enter BIONDELLO, *with* LUCENTIO *and* BIANCA.

BION. O, we are spoil'd ; and yonder he is ! Deny him, forswear
  him, or else we are all undone.
      [exeunt BIONDELLO, TRANIO, *and* PEDANT, *as fast as may be.*
LUC. *[kneeling.]* Pardon, sweet father.
VIN.   Lives my sweet son ?
BIAN. Pardon, dear father.
BAP.   How hast thou offended ?   100
  Where is Lucentio ?
LUC.   Here's Lucentio,
  Right son to the right Vincentio,
  That have by marriage made thy daughter mine,
  While counterfeit supposes blear'd thine eyne.
GRE. Here's packing, with a witness, to deceive us all !   105
VIN. Where is that damned villain, Tranio,
  That fac'd and brav'd me in this matter so ?
BAP. Why, tell me, is not this my Cambio ?
BIAN. Cambio is chang'd into Lucentio.
LUC. Love wrought these miracles. Bianca's love   110
  Made me exchange my state with Tranio,
  While he did bear my countenance in the town ;
  And happily I have arrived at the last
  Unto the wished haven of my bliss.
  What Tranio did, myself enforc'd him to ;   115
  Then pardon him, sweet father, for my sake.
VIN. I'll slit the villain's nose that would have sent me to the gaol.
BAP. *[to* LUCENTIO.*]* But do you hear, sir ?
  Have you married my daughter without asking my good will ?
VIN. Fear not, Baptista ; we will content you, go to ; but I will in
  to be revenged for this villainy.   *[exit.*
BAP. And I to sound the depth of this knavery.   *[exit.*
LUC. Look not pale, Bianca ; thy father will not frown.
      [exeunt LUCENTIO *and* BIANCA.
GRE. My cake is dough, but I'll in among the rest ;   125
  Out of hope of all but my share of the feast.   *[exit.*
KATH. Husband, let's follow to see the end of this ado.
PET. First kiss me, Kate, and we will.
KATH. What, in the midst of the street ?

PET. What, art thou asham'd of me ?   130
KATH. No, sir ; God forbid ; but asham'd to kiss.
PET. Why, then, let's home again.   Come, sirrah, let's away.
KATH. Nay, I will give thee a kiss ; now pray thee, love, stay.
PET. Is not this well ?   Come, my sweet Kate :
   Better once than never, for never too late.   [*exeunt.*

SCENE II. *Lucentio's house.*

Enter BAPTISTA, VINCENTIO, GREMIO, *the* PEDANT, LUCENTIO, BIANCA, PETRUCHIO, KATHERINA, HORTENSIO, *and* WIDOW. *The* SERVING-MEN *with* TRANIO, BIONDELLO, *and* GRUMIO, *bringing in a banquet.*

SCENE II
*Interior. Lucentio's
House. Night.*
GREMIO, PEDANT,
TRANIO, BIONDELLO
and GRUMIO
discovered. The rest
enter.

LUC. At last, though long, our jarring notes agree ;
   And time it is when raging war is done
   To smile at scapes and perils overblown.
   My fair Bianca, bid my father welcome,
   While I with self-same kindness welcome thine.   5
   Brother Petruchio, sister Katherina,
   And thou, Hortensio, with thy loving widow,
   Feast with the best, and welcome to my house.
   My banquet is to close our stomachs up
   After our great good cheer.   Pray you, sit down ;   10
   For now we sit to chat as well as eat.   [*they sit.*
PET. Nothing but sit and sit, and eat and eat !
BAP. Padua affords this kindness, son Petruchio.
PET. Padua affords nothing but what is kind.
HOR. For both our sakes I would that word were true.   15
PET. Now, for my life, Hortensio fears his widow.
WID. Then never trust me if I be afeard.
PET. You are very sensible, and yet you miss my sense :
   I mean Hortensio is afeard of you.
WID. He that is giddy thinks the world turns round.   20
PET. Roundly replied.
KATH. Mistress, how mean you that ?
WID. Thus I conceive by him.
PET. Conceives by me !   How likes Hortensio that ?
HOR. My widow says thus she conceives her tale.
PET. Very well mended.   Kiss him for that, good widow.   25
KATH. ' He that is giddy thinks the world turns round.'
   I pray you tell me what you meant by that.
WID. Your husband, being troubled with a shrew,
   Measures my husband's sorrow by his woe ;
   And now you know my meaning.   30
KATH. A very mean meaning.
WID.   Right, I mean you.
KATH. And I am mean, indeed, respecting you.
PET. To her, Kate !
HOR. To her, widow !
PET. A hundred marks, my Kate does put her down.   35
HOR. That's my office.
PET. Spoke like an officer—ha' to thee, lad.   [*drinks to* HORTENSIO.
BAP. How likes Gremio these quick-witted folks ?
GRE. Believe me, sir, they butt together well.

BIAN. Head and butt !   An hasty-witted body   40
 Would say your head and butt were head and horn.
VIN. Ay, mistress bride, hath that awakened you ?
BIAN. Ay, but not frighted me ; therefore I'll sleep again.
PET. Nay, that you shall not ; since you have begun,
 Have at you for a bitter jest or two.   45
BIAN. Am I your bird ?   I mean to shift my bush,
 And then pursue me as you draw your bow.
 You are welcome all.   [exeunt BIANCA, KATHERINA, and WIDOW
PET. She hath prevented me.   Here, Signior Tranio,
 This bird you aim'd at, though you hit her not ;   50
 Therefore a health to all that shot and miss'd.
TRA. O, sir, Lucentio slipp'd me like his greyhound,
 Which runs himself, and catches for his master.
PET. A good swift simile, but something currish.
TRA. 'Tis well, sir, that you hunted for yourself ;   55
 'Tis thought your deer does hold you at a bay.
BAP. O, O, Petruchio !   Tranio hits you now.
LUC. I thank thee for that gird, good Tranio.
HOR. Confess, confess ; hath he not hit you here ?
PET. 'A has a little gall'd me, I confess ;   60
 And, as the jest did glance away from me,
 'Tis ten to one it maim'd you two outright.
BAP. Now, in good sadness, son Petruchio,
 I think thou hast the veriest shrew of all.
PET. Well, I say no ; and therefore, for assurance,   65
 Let's each one send unto his wife,
 And he whose wife is most obedient,
 To come at first when he doth send for her,
 Shall win the wager which we will propose.
HOR. Content.   What's the wager ?
LUC.   Twenty crowns.   70
PET. Twenty crowns ?
 I'll venture so much of my hawk or hound,
 But twenty times so much upon my wife.
LUC. A hundred then.
HOR.   Content.
PET.   A match ! 'tis done.
HOR. Who shall begin ?
LUC.   That will I.   75
 Go, Biondello, bid your mistress come to me.
BION. I go.   [exit.
BAP. Son, I'll be your half Bianca comes.
LUC. I'll have no halves ; I'll bear it all myself.

Re-enter BIONDELLO.

 How now ! what news ?
BION.   Sir, my mistress sends you word   80
 That she is busy and she cannot come.
PET. How !   She's busy, and she cannot come !
 Is that an answer ?
GRE.   Ay, and a kind one too.
 Pray God, sir, your wife send you not a worse.
PET. I hope better.   85

HOR. Sirrah Biondello, go and entreat my wife
    To come to me forthwith.   *[exit* BIONDELLO.
PET.   O, ho ! entreat her !
    Nay, then she must needs come.
HOR.   I am afraid, sir,
    Do what you can, yours will not be entreated.

               Re-enter BIONDELLO.

    Now, where's my wife ?   90
BION. She says you have some goodly jest in hand :
    She will not come ; she bids you come to her.
PET. Worse and worse ; she will not come !   O vile,
    Intolerable, not to be endur'd !
    Sirrah Grumio, go to your mistress ;   95
    Say I command her come to me.   *[exit* GRUMIO.
HOR. I know her answer.
PET.   What ?
HOR.   She will not.
PET. The fouler fortune mine, and there an end.

               Re-enter KATHERINA.

BAP. Now, by my holidame, here comes Katherina !
KATH. What is your will, sir, that you send for me ?   100
PET. Where is your sister, and Hortensio's wife ?
KATH. They sit conferring by the parlour fire.
PET. Go, fetch them hither ; if they deny to come,
    Swinge me them soundly forth unto their husbands.
    Away, I say, and bring them hither straight.   *[exit* KATHERINA.
LUC. Here is a wonder, if you talk of a wonder.
HOR. And so it is.   I wonder what it bodes.
PET. Marry, peace it bodes, and love, and quiet life,
    An awful rule, and right supremacy ;
    And, to be short, what not that's sweet and happy.   110
BAP. Now fair befall thee, good Petruchio !
    The wager thou hast won ; and I will add
    Unto their losses twenty thousand crowns ;
    Another dowry to another daughter,
    For she is chang'd, as she had never been.   115
PET. Nay, I will win my wager better yet,
    And show more sign of her obedience,
    Her new-built virtue and obedience.

     Re-enter KATHERINA *with* BIANCA *and* WIDOW.

    See where she comes, and brings your froward wives
    As prisoners to her womanly persuasion.   120
    Katherine, that cap of yours becomes you not :
    Off with that bauble, throw it underfoot.   [KATHERINA *complies.*
WID. Lord, let me never have a cause to sigh
    Till I be brought to such a silly pass !
BIAN. Fie ! what a foolish duty call you this ?   125
LUC. I would your duty were as foolish too ;
    The wisdom of your duty, fair Bianca,
    Hath cost me a hundred crowns since supper-time !

BIAN. The more fool you for laying on my duty.
PET. Katherine, I charge thee, tell these headstrong women   130
    What duty they do owe their lords and husbands.
WID. Come, come, you're mocking ; we will have no telling.
PET. Come on, I say ; and first begin with her.
WID. She shall not.
PET. I say she shall.   And first begin with her.   135
KATH. Fie, fie ! unknit that threatening unkind brow,
    And dart not scornful glances from those eyes
    To wound thy lord, thy king, thy governor.
    It blots thy beauty as frosts do bite the meads.
    Confounds thy fame as whirlwinds shake fair buds,   140
    And in no sense is meet or amiable.
    A woman mov'd is like a fountain troubled—
    Muddy, ill-seeming, thick, bereft of beauty ;
    And while it is so, none so dry or thirsty
    Will deign to sip or touch one drop of it.   145
    Thy husband is thy lord, thy life, thy keeper,
    Thy head, thy sovereign ; one that cares for thee,
    And for thy maintenance commits his body
    To painful labour both by sea and land,
    To watch the night in storms, the day in cold,   150
    Whilst thou liest warm at home, secure and safe
    And craves no other tribute at thy hands
    But love, fair looks, and true obedience—
    Too little payment for so great a debt.
    Such duty as the subject owes the prince,   155
    Even such a woman oweth to her husband ;
    And when she is froward, peevish, sullen, sour,
    And not obedient to his honest will,
    What is she but a foul contending rebel
    And graceless traitor to her loving lord ?   160
    I am asham'd that women are so simple
    To offer war where they should kneel for peace ;
    Or seek for rule, supremacy, and sway,
    When they are bound to serve, love, and obey.
    Why are our bodies soft and weak and smooth,   165
    Unapt to toil and trouble in the world,
    But that our soft conditions and our hearts
    Should well agree with our external parts ?
    Come, come, you froward and unable worms !
    My mind hath been as big as one of yours,   170
    My heart as great, my reason haply more,
    To bandy word for word and frown for frown ;
    But now I see our lances are but straws,
    Our strength as weak, our weakness past compare,
    That seeming to be most which we indeed least are.   175
    Then vail your stomachs, for it is no boot,
    And place your hands below your husband's foot ;
    In token of which duty, if he please,
    My hand is ready, may it do him ease.
PET. Why, there's a wench !   Come on, and kiss me, Kate.   180
LUC. Well, go thy ways, old lad, for thou shalt ha't.

VIN. 'Tis a good hearing when children are toward.
LUC. But a harsh hearing when women are froward.
PET. Come, Kate, we'll to bed.
    We three are married, but you two are sped.   185
    [*to* LUCENTIO.]   'Twas I won the wager, though you hit the white ;
    And being a winner, God give you good night !
                [*exeunt* PETRUCHIO *and* KATHERINA.
HOR. Now go thy ways ; thou hast tam'd a curst shrow.
LUC. 'Tis a wonder, by your leave, she will be tam'd so.   [*exeunt.*

> Lines 186–187
> omitted.
>
> PETRUCHIO and
> KATHERINA remain.
> Song sheets are
> handed out. Psalm
> 128, 'O blest is he
> that fears the Lord',
> is sung by the
> assembled company,
> under the direction of
> GREMIO.

GLOSSARY

Graham May

Difficult phrases are listed under the most important or most difficult word in them. If no such word stands out, they are listed under the first word.

Words appear in the form they take in the text. If they occur in several forms, they are listed under the root form (singular for nouns, infinitive for verbs).

Line references are given only when the same word is used with different meanings, and when there are puns.

Line numbers of prose passages are counted from the last numbered line before the line referred to (since the numbers given do not always correspond to those in this edition).

A, in, I ii 191, IV v 1; on, II i 316; in the, IV iii 92; 'see the church a your back', see the church behind you, i.e. see you safely married

'A, (often =) he

ABANDON'D, banished

ABOUT, at large, everywhere, IV ii 87; see ROUNDLY, IV iv 102

ABOVE, i.e. on some form of upper stage, I i 242 *Stage Direction*

ABROAD, i.e. making a sea voyage on board a ship (some editions read 'aboard')

ABUS'D, ill-treated

ACCEPT OF, accept

ACCOMPLISHED, performed

ACCORD, harmony

ACHIEVE, (often =) win

ACQUAINTANCE, friends that you have

ACTION, general behaviour, bearing, *Induction* i 130; see BRING, III ii 230

ADO, trouble, disturbance

ADONIS, (allusion to the myth, recounted by Ovid in his *Metamorphoses* x 520–739, that Cytherea (Venus, the classical goddess of love, called 'Cytherea' because of her traditional association with the island of Cythera) fell in love with a youth called Adonis who was killed by a wild boar he was hunting. When Venus found the body, she transformed his blood into a flower – the anemone)

ADVERSARIES, i.e. lawyers on opposite sides of a case

ADVICE, careful reflection

ADVIS'D, aware that

AEACIDES, the descendant of Aeacus (i.e. Ajax Telamonius, whose grandfather was Aeacus, and who was one of the Greek heroes of the Trojan War; Lucentio has either moved on to the next line of Ovid's *Heroides*, which begins 'Illic Aeacides . . .', or is referring to Ovid's *Metamorphoses* xiii 27–28 in an attempt to throw Hortensio off the scent)

AFEARD, afraid

AFFABILITY, kind and gentle friendliness

AFFECT, find pleasing, I i 40; love, II i 14

AFFECTED AS, inclined as, in agreement with

AFFECTION TO, love for

AFFECTION'S EDGE, see REMOVES

AFFIED, 'We be affied, and . . . stand', We may be betrothed, and such legal arrangements be made as shall be agreeable to both parties

AFFORDS, can supply, *Induction* i 102; offers, V ii 13f.

AFTER, go after, III ii 123

AGAIN, 'again to take it up', to take it up again

AGAINST, see BIAS, IV v 25; 'against you come', in preparation for your coming

AGENOR, see DAUGHTER OF AGENOR

AGLET-BABY, small figure serving as a tag on a lacing-cord

AGREE, are in harmony, V ii 1

AIM'D OF, guessed by

ALARUMS, sounds to warn of danger, such as

peals of church bells, trumpet calls, shouts, etc.

AL'CE, Alice

ALCIDES' TWELVE, i.e. Hercules's twelve 'Labours' (Hercules was a descendant of Alceus; see HERCULES)

ALE-WIFE, a woman who kept an ale-house

ALL, entirely, I ii 237; 'all in all', i.e. fundamental to any agreement; 'all one', the same thing; 'all amort', totally dispirited

ALLA NOSTRA . . . PETRUCIO, welcome to our house, my most honoured friend Signior Petruchio

ALLOTS, allot (the old plural)

ALOFT, i.e. on some form of upper stage

ALONE, see HOPE, I ii 243; see BEING, II i 296

AM, i.e. who was, II i 268

AMAZ'D, bewildered

AMAZED, bewildered

AMENDS, amendment, recovery in health

AMISS, inaccurately, II i 283

AMORT, see ALL

AN, if; 'an it like you', if it pleases you

ANCIENT, of long standing, I ii 45; 'ancient thoughts', i.e. former capacity to think reasonably; 'ancient angel', i.e. a fellow of the good old stamp ('angel' = a gold coin on which was stamped a design depicting the archangel Michael)

AND, see ENOUGH, I i 127; 'and all one', (perhaps) (i) and just the very same, (ii) but no matter

ANGEL, see ANCIENT

ANNA, (allusion to the Latin poet Virgil's story, told in his *Aeneid* iv 8–30, of how Dido, Queen of the city of Carthage on the coast of North Africa, confided in her sister Anna that she had fallen in love with her guest the Trojan ₁rince Aeneas who was passing through her domain on his way from the fallen city of Troy to found a kingdom in Italy)

ANON, Soon, immediately

ANSWER, 'answer them', i.e. echo back their cries

ANSWERABLE TO, properly corresponding to

AN'T, if it

APACE, swiftly

APOLLO, Greek god of healing, archery, and music

APPENDIX, addition, i.e. bride (metaphor from printing)

APPLE, 'As much . . . apple . . . oyster', (proverbial)

APPLY, devote myself to

APPOINTED HOURS, i.e. given a time-table

APPROV'D, proved, found reliable

APT, willing, quick

ARGOSY, merchant vessel of the largest size and burden (a term especially used to denote the large merchant ships of Ragusa and Venice)

ARISTOTLE, Greek philosopher, pupil of Plato and tutor of Alexander the Great, whose ethical treatises (the *Nichomachean Ethics* and *Eudemian ethics*) advocate the subordination of the pursuit of pleasure, fame, and wealth to the contemplation of philosophic truth through the cultivation of rational thought

ARMS, see LOSE, II i 218, II i 220

ARRAS COUNTERPOINTS, counterpanes of arras tapestry (a rich tapestry fabric in which figures and scenes are woven in colours; a hanging screen of this was often placed round the walls of a room)

ARRAY, dress, clothing

ART, 'The Art of Love', (i.e. the *Ars Amatoria* (*The Art of Love*), a poem by the Latin poet Ovid in which love is wittily presented as if it were a science)

AS, So that, *Induction* i 68; i.e. if he wishes to, *Induction* i 107; That, I i 33; as if, II i 158, V i 14; as to, I ii 247; see THINK, IV iii 113; 'As beaten', As if driven, as if they felt themselves to be driven; 'as yourself', as if you yourself, I ii 153; 'as weak', i.e. as weak as straws; 'As who should say', As if to say; 'as she had never been', as if she had never existed, out of all recognition

ASHORE, (Padua is in fact an inland city without a coastline), I i 42

ASK, 'ask him', ask him for, III i 172; 'ask the banns', have the banns read ('banns' = public notice given in church of an intended marriage in order that anyone who may know of any impediment to the marriage's taking place may lodge an objection)

ASKANCE, scornfully

ASKETH, requires, demands

ASSURANCE, i.e. of the dowry which you have promised (see LET), II i 379; II i 388; see PASS, IV ii 117; see AFFIED, IV iv 49; see TAKE, IV iv 89; proof, V ii 65; 'counterfeit assurance', counterfeit legal settlement

ASSURE, guarantee, convey property by legal deed (legal term), II i 335, II i 337; guarantee (see 'assure . . . widowhood'), II i 371; 'assure . . . widowhood', guarantee that she will receive her rightful share of the estate if she becomes a widow ('widowhood' = the estate settled upon a widow)

AT, see HAND, I ii 223; 'at the merest loss', see CRIED: 'at hand', close at hand, IV i 102

ATTEND, await, II i 167

AUGHT, 'for aught I see', for anything that I can see

AWFUL RULE, order commanding due respect

BACARE, stand back (jocular pseudo-Latin made up from 'back' + the Latin infinitive ending '-are', and perhaps taken from the proverb 'Backare, quoth Mortimer to his sow')

BAGGAGE, good-for-nothing woman, strumpet

BAGS, i.e. money bags

BALK LOGIC, chop logic

BALM, anoint, bathe

BANDY, exchange (as a ball is hit to and fro in tennis)

BANNS, see ASK

BANQUET, a light dessert of wine, fruit, and sweetmeats

BAR IN LAW, legal impediment (i.e. Baptista's refusal to allow them to court Bianca)

BARE-FOOT, see DANCE BARE-FOOT

BARS, prevents

BASTA, Enough

BATE, 'bate and beat', flutter and flap the wings impatiently

BAY, 'hold you at a bay', turn to make a stand against you (a hunting term used to describe a stag turning on the pursuing dogs and defending itself with its horns)

BE, are, III ii 201, IV i 104; see REMEMB'RED, IV iii 96; 'be it', if it be, II i 123; 'be with you', i.e. be after you (to punish you), IV i 151

BEAR, must bear, Induction i 108; carry burdens, II i 198; (i) bear children, (ii) support a man during sexual intercourse (pun and innuendo), II i 199; endure, III i 15; keep, IV iii 49; 'bear my countenance', take on my identity

BEARING, see PORT, III i 34–35

BEARS, lies (nautical term), V i 8; 'bears me fair in hand', treats me encouragingly (with a suggestion that she is deceiving him)

BEAST, 'I am no beast', (i.e. Curtis feels that, as Grumio called himself a 'beast' and called Curtis his 'fellow', he implied that Curtis himself is a 'beast')

BEASTLY, lewdly, in an animal fashion

BEAT, see BATE, IV i 180

BEATEN, 'beaten out of door', driven out of the house

BECAUSE, In order that, I i 179

BECK, nod (of command)

BECOME, adorn, grace, II i 251; befit, suit, IV v 32; 'Vincentio's son . . . virtuous deeds', It shall well befit Vincentio's son, brought up in Florence, to fulfil ('serve') all the hopes men have for him by adorning his inherited fortune with virtuous deeds

BECOMES, suits, befits, I ii 85, V ii 121; 'as becomes', in the proper manner (i.e. as if Tranio were in fact myself), I i 227

BEETLE-HEADED, block-headed ('beetle' = a heavy mallet)

BEFALL, see FAIR

BEFORE, ahead, IV i 111; i.e. earlier (pun), IV i 112

BEGNAWN WITH, eaten away by

BEHOLDING, beholden, indebted, I ii 270; see KINDLY, II i 77

BEING, 'being alone', when we were alone

BELIKE, probably; perhaps, it seems likely, I i 103; probably, no doubt, IV iii 103

BELONGS, belong, befit, II i 347; 'to thee belongs', you rightfully deserve

BEMETE, measure, i.e. beat

BEMOIL'D, covered with mud

BEN VENUTO, welcome, i.e. host (Italian)

BERGAMO, Italian town twenty-five miles to the north-east of Milan

BESEEM, befit

BESET WITH, surrounded by

BESPEAK, order

BEST, the best thing you could do would be to, IV iii 76; see MAKE, IV iii 100; see WERE, V i 13

BESTOW, give in marriage, I i 50

BESTOW'D, married

BESTRAUGHT, distracted, mad

BESTREW, spread coverings (perhaps rushes) upon

BETHINK THEE, remember, recollect

BETTER, 'Better once . . . too late', i.e. Better to have changed for the better at some time ('once') than never to have done so, for it is never too late to change for the better (Petruchio blends two proverbs: 'Better late than never' and 'It is never too late to mend')

BIAS, 'against the bias', against its natural course (a 'bowl' generally has a 'bias' = a lead weight placed off-centre within it which causes its path to be curved rather than straight)

BID, asked, IV iii 94; ordered, IV iii 125f.

BIG, threatening (said, not to Katherina, to whom it really applies, but to the wedding guests), III ii 224; haughty, arrogant, V ii 170

BILL, (i) note (see IV iii 128), (ii) bill of indictment, accusation, IV iii 142; weapon (long-handled pike; pun), IV iii 147

BILLS, 'bills for money by exchange', bills of exchange, promissory notes

BIRD, i.e. prey at which you are shooting arrows, V ii 46

BITTER, shrewd, sharp, V ii 45

BLAME, see TO, IV iii 48

BLEAR'D THINE EYNE, dimmed (i.e. deceived) your eyes ('eyne' = eyes)

BLOTS, disfigures

BLOW (n.), blasting noise, I ii 205; (v), 'Love is not . . . blow our nails together', i.e. Our love of women (i.e. rivalry over Bianca) is not so great, Hortensio, that we cannot wait patiently ('blow our nails' is the equivalent of 'twiddle our thumbs')

BLUE COATS, the usual dress of menservants

BLUNT, rude, III ii 14

BOARD, i.e. accost, woo (naval term meaning 'to come alongside a ship in order to attack it and climb aboard it')

BODES, portends, presages

BOLD, impolite; imprudent, II i 86; 'be bold with you', be impolite to you; 'Am bold to show', Take the liberty of showing

BOLDNESS, impudence

BONNY, fine, big

BOOKS, (i) heraldic registers, (ii) 'good books', i.e. favour (pun), II i 221

BOOT, 'it is no boot', it is of no use or profit

BOOT-HOSE, stocking for wearing under boots

BORROW, (pun on 'credit' of IV i 90; see CREDIT)

BOSS'D, embossed, studded

BOTS, intestinal worms (larvae of the botfly)

BOTTOM, ball (a 'bottom' = the bobbin on which a ball of thread was wound)

BOW'D, bent

BOWL, ball in a game of bowls

BOY, (here, term of contempt, applicable to both sexes), Induction i 11

BRACH, bitch hound (some editions read 'Breathe' = allow to rest, or 'Broach' =

'bleed', i.e. let the blood of as a cure for exhaustion), Induction i 15

BRAV'D, defied; (i) provided fine clothes for, (ii) defied (pun), IV iii 124

BRAVE (adj.), i.e. finely dressed; (v.), (i) provide fine clothes for, (ii) defy, IV iii 124

BRAVELY, splendidly, I ii 214 Stage Direction; finely dressed, IV iii 54

BRAVES, defiant insults

BRAV'RY, finery

BREAK, 'break her to', train her to play (as a wild horse is 'broken' = tamed); 'break a jest', play a practical joke

BREATHE, pause for breath, i.e. remain for a time, I i 8

BREATHED, strong of breath

BREECHING SCHOLAR, schoolboy who is (i) in short trousers, i.e. young, (ii) liable to be whipped if he does wrong

BRIDE IT, play a bride

BRIEF, 'in brief', to be brief

BRIEFER, see SORT

BRING, 'bring mine action on', (i) attack, (ii) bring legal proceedings against

BROACH'D, I began to speak about

BROIL'D, grilled, cooked over coals

BROKE, i.e. bruised and bleeding, II i 140 Stage Direction

BROOK'D PARLE, allowed us to speak together

BUCKLER, shield, defend (a 'buckler' = a small shield)

BUGS, bugbears, bogeymen (see FEAR)

BURDEN (n.), (in music) ground-bass accompaniment, undersong, I ii 66; (v.), (i) lie heavy on (see BEAR), (ii) make accusations against, II i 201

BURST, broken

BURTON HEATH, (perhaps Barton-on-the-Heath, a Warwickshire village about sixteen miles from Stratford)

BUT, (often =) only, merely; indeed, Induction ii 76; see BLOW, I i 107; except, II i 167 Stage Direction; Not other than, II i 239; see HOW, II i 274; see SEE, II i 399; unless, III i 60, IV iv 2; see NO, III ii 8; nothing but, III ii 22; than, IV i 13, IV ii 2; other than, V ii 14; 'a bed but cold', a cold bed indeed in which; 'but of all', but especially, I ii 2; 'but to', if not for, I ii 195; 'I'll plead . . . but you shall', I'll even plead your case to him myself in order that you may have him; 'but as I find', strictly in accordance with the facts as I find them; 'but that you are but newly come',

91

except for the fact that you have only just arrived; 'But that', unless, V ii 167

BUTT (n.), bottom, V ii 40; *see* HORN, V ii 41; (v.), 'butt together', butt each other

BUTTERY, store room for liquor (kept in butts) and other provisions

BUZZ, (pun on 'be' = bee, implying that her words are no more than senseless buzzing)

BUZZARD, (i) kind of hawk of little use for falconry, (ii) worthless, ignorant, stupid person, II i 205; cockchafer (*see* TURTLE), II i 207

BY, as a result of, *Induction* i 68; to one side, I ii 139, IV ii 5; 'by the year', *see* DUCATS; 'by this', by this time, IV v 62

CAKE, *see* DOUGH; 'cake's dough', *see* DOUGH

CALLS, (second person singular), IV i 89

CAMBIO, (Italian for 'exchange')

CAME, were to come, I ii 243; 'we came in', i.e. our family arrived in this country

CANDLE-CASES, i.e. so old as to only be fit for storing candles (or candle-ends) in

CANOPIES, coverings suspended over a throne, bed, etc.

CAPARISON'D, outfitted ('caparison' = covering, often ornamented, spread over the saddle or harness of a horse)

CARDMAKER, a maker of 'cards' (= metal combs for separating and combing-out the fibres of woollen fleeces in preparation for spinning them)

CARE, 'her care should be', she would take care

CARELESS, regardless

CAROUSE, 'carouse full measure', drink deep toasts

CAROUSES, toasts

CAROUSING, drinking toasts

CARPETS LAID, (probably on tables and chests rather than on the floor)

CART (v.), (allusion to 'carting', the normal punishment for prostitution which involved the whipping of the accused woman while she was drawn through the streets on a cart)

CARV'D, slashed (*see* SLEEVE)

CAST, 'cast on no water', (allusion to the popular round-song 'Scotland's burning, Scotland's burning, / See yonder! See yonder! / Fire, fire! Fire, fire! / Cast on water! Cast on water!')

CAUSE, matter, business, IV iv 26

CAVIL, 'but a cavil', merely a cavilling objection

CENSER, perfuming pan with a perforated lid

'CERNS, 'what 'cerns it you', what business is it of yours

CHAFE, (i) irritate, (ii) excite, inflame

CHAFED, irritated

CHANCE (n.), happening, event, I ii 44

CHANGES, (perhaps a pun on the moon's 'changes', i.e. its waning and waxing; there may be a further irony, too, for the moon was thought to govern the moods of lunatics)

CHANGING, i.e. loving someone else

CHAPELESS, without a 'chape' (= a metal plate on the end of a sword's sheath)

CHARG'D, ordered

CHARGE (n.), expense, I ii 212; (v.), order

CHARM, i.e. give him strict orders, I i 204; bewitch (into silence), IV ii 58

CHATTELS, movable possessions; 'my goods, my chattels . . . any thing', (allusion to the Tenth Commandment; Petruchio is hinting that the wedding guests are coveting his wife)

CHECKS, restraints, councels of moderation (*see* ARISTOTLE)

CHEER, hospitable entertainment, *Induction* ii 99; food and drink, III ii 182; welcome, entertainment, IV iv 70; reception, entertainment (at Baptista's house), V ii 10; 'what cheer', how are you (Katherina puns on 'cheer' = hospitable welcome, entertainment), IV iii 37; 'cheer is toward', entertainment is in preparation

CHIDE, scold

CHOICE (adj.), chosen, appointed, I ii 233

CHOK'D, silenced

CHOLER, bile (one of the four bodily 'humours' or fluids (blood, phlegm, choler, and melancholy or black choler) by the relative proportions of which a person's physical and mental qualities and disposition were believed to be determined)

CHOLERIC, productive of anger, hot-tempered (*see* CHOLER)

CHOOSE, 'cannot choose', i.e. must, is bound to; 'You shall not choose but', You must; 'I hope I may choose', i.e. I am not subject to your orders

CICELY HACKET, *see* MARIAN HACKET

CIRCUMSTANCES, details, IV ii 119; *see* LEAVE, V i 23

CLEAR, cheerful, serene

CLEF, key (i.e., perhaps, 'love')

CLOSE, 'close our stomachs up', i.e. make a fitting end to our meal (pun on 'put an end to our common propensity for anger' ('stomachs')); 'close' (adv.), secretly, *Induction* i 125

COCKLE, cockleshell

COCK'S PASSION, by God's suffering (oath)

COLD, i.e. miserable, poor (*see* CHEER), IV iii 37; 'cold comfort', i.e. discomfort (she will strike him)

COLDLY, 'so coldly', i.e. anything but peremptorily, like one who is benumbed with cold

COMB, i.e. beat

COMBLESS, with comb cut down, i.e. gentle

COME, *see* ASHORE, I i 42; 'come of', descended from, I i 13; 'come roundly', speak bluntly, plainly; 'come you now with', i.e. and do you now come out with the assertion that you said; 'come again', (i) come back, (ii) renew the debate, II i 215; 'come by', get, find, IV i 7

COMES, *see* KNOCK, I ii 15

COMET, (allusion to the belief that comets were omens of disaster)

COMMAND, *see* WHOM, II i 250; service, IV iv 85

COMMANDED, forced, acted, *Induction* i 123

COMMEND, 'commend me', give my greetings, good wishes

COMMODITY, piece of saleable goods (which)

COMMUNE, talk over

COMONTY, (Sly's mistake for 'comedy')

COMPANY, 'for company', together

COMPARE, comparison

COMPASS'D, circular

COMPOUND, settle

'CON TUTTO . . . TROVATO', (Italian) with all my heart well met

CONCEIT, idea, meaning

CONCEIV'D, *see* BECOME

CONCEIVE, understand the situation, I ii 267; 'Thus I conceive by him', That is what I take him for (*see* CONCEIVES)

CONCEIVES, interprets (pun), V ii 24; 'Conceives by', Is made pregnant by (pun; *see* CONCEIVE)

CONCERNETH, 'But to her love concerneth . . . liking', But it is important to us to add her father's approval to her (i.e. Bianca's) own love for you

CONDITIONS, qualities

CONFERENCE, conversation

CONFERRING, chatting

CONFESS, admit (to having specified), IV iii 137

CONFORMABLE, tractable, compliant

CONFOUNDS, destroys

CONGEAL'D, (allusion to the contemporary medical belief that melancholy thickens the blood)

CONSENT, i.e. her father's approval, III ii 133; i.e. my consent, IV iv 47; 'With one consent', in entire agreement

CONSERVES, candied fruits; 'conserves of beef', preserved (i.e. salted) beef

CONSOLATION, comfort

CONSTRUE, analyse the grammar of (or 'translate') a sentence

CONSUME, 'consume the thing . . . fury', burn out and hence exhaust what caused and fuelled the fire (i.e. Katherina's shrewishness; *see* WIND)

CONTENT, 'content you . . . discontent', take pleasure in my discomfort; 'content ye', be content; 'Content you', Be calm

CONTENTED, 'so contented', i.e. willing to see it and accept it as well cooked

CONTENTS, satisfied me, I i 158; pleases, IV iii 174

CONTRIVE, spend, pass (time)

CONYCATCHING, rabbit-catching, i.e. trickery, evasion (perhaps with an allusion to Grumio's apparent fondness for 'catches' = round-songs)

CONY-CATCH'D, duped

COOL, to cool

COPATAIN, high-crowned, sugar-loaf

CORAL, of the colour of red coral

COUNTENANCE (n.), 'under my countenance', in my person, by pretending to be me; 'bear my countenance', take on my identity; (v.), show respect to, IV i 85

COUNTERPOINTS, *see* ARRAS

COUNT'NANCE, outward appearance, meaning, I i 223

COUNTRYMAN, 'What countryman', i.e. Where do you come from

COUPLE, leash together, *Induction* i 16

COURSE, hunt hares (with greyhounds), *Induction* ii 45

COURTESY, (perhaps 'curtsy'), *Induction* i 112; a courteous act, IV ii 91

COURT'SY, a courteous act

COVENANTS, documents of formal and legal agreement

COXCOMB, a cap in the shape of a cock's comb which a court jester often possessed as part of his uniform

COY, disdainful

COZEN, cheat; cheat (by making the ceremony invalid in some way), III ii 164

CRAB, (i) (bitter) crab apple, (ii) bad-tempered person (pun), II i 226f.

CRACK, roar explosively (like a gun), thunder

CRACK-HEMP, scoundrel who deserves to be hung, 'gallows-bird'

CRAVE THE DAY, enquire as to the date

CRAVEN, a cock that will not fight

CREDIT (n.), reputation; (v.), do honour to, IV i 90; provide credit for (Grumio's pun), IV i 91

CREST, (i) heraldic device carried above the shield or helmet, (ii) comb, as on a bird's head

CRIED, 'cried upon . . . loss', i.e. bayed out (that he had found the scent) when it had been completely lost ('merest' = uttermost, most complete)

CROSS (adj.), given to contradiction, II i 242; (v.), contradict, annoy, II i 28

CROSS'D, interrupted, IV i 63; opposed, contradicted, IV v 10

CROSSING, contradicting, hindering

CROWNS, coins (which were worth five shillings apiece)

CRUPPER, leather hoop which passed under a horse's tail to prevent the saddle slipping

CULLION, base fellow

CUM PRIVILEGIO . . . SOLUM, (Latin) with the sole right to print (inscription frequently found on the title pages of Elizabethan books, probably alluding to the fact that many printers claimed exclusive rights to print certain editions or types of books (there is a pun: 'imprimendum' = (i) printing, (ii) 'pressing upon', i.e. stamping one's image on someone by getting them with child)

CUNNING, (adj.), skilful; (n.), skill, art, *Induction* i 90; see FAIL, II i 403

CUR, dog

CURIOUS, over-fastidious about details

CURIOUSLY, elaborately, painstakingly

CURRISH, (i) dog-like, i.e. base, (ii) having reference to a dog (pun)

CURST, shrewish, waspish, ill-tempered

CURSTER, more shrewish

CURSTEST, most shrewish

CURTSY, 'curtsy . . . legs', (a sign of submission: to put the 'best' leg forward was a sign of defiance)

CUSTARD-COFFIN, crust of pastry over or in which a custard was baked (perhaps with a pun on 'costard' = head)

CUSTOM, 'without my custom', without doing any trade with me

CYPRESS, made of the wood of the cypress tree

CYTHEREA, *see* ADONIS

DAINTIES, 'dainties are all Kates', (pun on 'dainties' = delicacies, and 'cates' = delicacies)

DALLY, trifle delayingly

DAM, mother (a word usually used of quadrupeds, and contemptuous when applied to human beings), III ii 152; 'the devil's dam', the devil's mother (proverbially more evil than the devil himself)

DAME, mistress, madam, (a rebuke is implied)

DANCE BARE-FOOT, i.e. be unmarried (it was traditional for an unmarried elder sister to dance barefoot at the wedding of a younger sister)

DAPHNE, (allusion to the myth, told in the Latin poet Ovid's *Metamorphoses* i 452–567, that Cupid (the Roman boy-god of love), in order to show his power to the scornful Apollo (the Roman god of music), caused Apollo to fall in love with Daphne (a daughter of the river-god Peneus) whilst making her detest him in return. Apollo pursued her; but she fled and her father rescued her by turning her into a laurel tree)

DAUGHTER OF AGENOR, (allusion to the myth, told by the Latin poet Ovid in his *Metamorphoses* ii 846–875, that Jupiter (the King of the Roman gods) fell in love with Europa, the daughter of Agenor, King of Tyre. To win her, Jupiter changed himself into a bull and kneeled before her; she mounted on his back, and he immediately carried her off to Crete)

DEAR, (i) dearly, (ii) expensively (pun)

DECEITFUL, DECEIVING, pretend, sham

DECK, *see* BECOME, I i 16; adorn, IV iii 60

DECLINING, 'with declining . . . bosom', with his head drooping on his chest

DEEDS, (i) actions that, (ii) (perhaps) legal deeds that, II i 334

DEEP, i.e. ocean

DEEPER, more profound, obscure (possibly with an innuendo), IV iii 157

DEEPLY, *see* SOUNDED, II i 192

DEER, (pun on 'dear' = wife), V ii 56

DEMI-CANNON, large cannon (of a bore of about six and a half inches; *see* SLEEVE)

DENIER, very small French coin (worth one tenth of a sou)

DENY, refuse, II i 178; V ii 103; 'Deny him, forswear him', i.e. Deny on oath that he is Vincentio

DESCRIED, seen, recognised

DESPITE, 'in despite', i.e. in spite of his inability to weep

DESPITEFUL, spiteful

DEVICE, scheme, I i 188; stratagem, I ii 132

DEVOTE, devoted

DIAN, Diana (the classical goddess of the moon, hunting, and chastity)

DIAPER, towel

DID, i.e. indeed I did, IV iii 96

DIGRESS, (i) go out of my way, (ii) deviate from my promise (or from the plan to 'buy apparel 'gainst the wedding day', see II i 306–307)

DINNER-TIME, i.e. around noon

DIRECTION, 'had direction', was given instructions

DISCOMFITED, dejected, thrown into confusion (originally 'routed in battle')

DISEASE, i.e. disease of mind

DISQUIET, upset, ill-tempered

DISSEMBLE, lie, II i 9

DISTILLED WATERS, (i.e., perhaps, perfumed liquids made from flowers and herbs)

DO, 'How do you', i.e. How are all the family, I ii 22; 'do little good upon', have little effect upon; 'What have you to do', What is it to do with you; 'What hast . . . do', What concern is it of yours; 'do it', may it do, IV iii 51; 'do him ease', give him satisfaction

DOES, is, III ii 89

DOFF, take off (of clothing)

DOG-WEARY, dog-tired, exhausted

DOING, see FAIN

DOLE, lot (see HAPPY)

DOMINEER, carouse, feast riotously

DONE, finished (see TUNE), III i 23

DOOR, see BEATEN, Induction ii 83

DOTARD, senile old fool

DOUBLETS, jackets

DOUGH, 'Our cake's . . . sides', (proverbial expression of failure, i.e. we have both equally failed); 'My cake is dough', I have failed miserably (see above)

DOWER, dowry; 'greatest dower', the greatest dowry

DRAWN, drawn up, II i 125

DRESS, prepare, IV iii 40

DRESSER, sideboard

DRINK, see HOLD, IV iv 17

DROOP, feel sad

DUCATS, 'two thousand ducats . . . land', fertile land which brings in a yearly income of two thousand ducats (a 'ducat' = a Venetian gold coin worth somewhere between a quarter and a half of a contemporary pound sterling; two thousand ducats would therefore have been worth between five hundred and a thousand contemporary pounds sterling, or at least £13,000 in modern money)

DULCET, sweetly melodious

DUMPS, 'in your dumps', are you downcast

DURST, dare, IV i 147; dared to, IV ii 12

DUTY, i.e. expression of respect, Induction i 80; i.e. respectful actions, Induction i 111; dutiful service, IV i 110; dutiful obedience, V ii 125ff.; obedience, V ii 131, V ii 178; 'Do thy duty . . . duty', Do your duty (by making a fire) and thus get your reward ('duty')

EASE, see DO

EAT, 'She eat', She ate, IV i 181

EATEN, see OATS

EDGE, see REMOVES

E'EN, even

E'ER, ever

EFFECTS, causes

EFFECTUAL, effective

EITHER, see HAND, II i 126

ELEVEN AND TWENTY, 'tricks eleven and twenty long', i.e. tricks which are exactly right (allusion to the card-game Trentuno (= Thirty-and-one); see I ii 32)

ELSE, (often =) otherwise; see WITLESS, II i 257

EMBOSS'D, foaming at the mouth (with exhaustion)

ENCOUNTER, manner of address, behaviour

END, 'and there an end', and that's that, that's an end of it

ENDUR'D, suffered, allowed, IV iii 75

ENOUGH, 'and money enough', i.e. provided her dowry were big enough

ENTERTAINMENT, hospitality, welcome; (see ENTRANCE), II i 54; see II i 141ff., III i 2

ENTERTAIN'ST, welcomest

ENTIRE, complete, sincere

ENTRANCE, 'for an entrance . . . entertainment', as an entrance fee for my hospitable reception ('entertainment')

ENTREATY, see UPON

ENVIOUS, malicious

ENVY, hate, feel jealous of

ERE, before; (see TUNE), III i 23; 'Or ere', Before

ERGO, therefore (pedantic latinism used in logical disputation)

ESTATE, social position, station

ESTEEM, reputation, IV v 63

EVENT, outcome

EWER, pitcher of water for washing hands

EWERS, *see* EWER

EXCHANGE, *see* BILLS, IV ii 89

EXECUTE, 'that thyself execute', that you yourself must perform

EYNE, eyes

FAC'D, (i) trimmed, (ii) defied (*see* FACE), IV iii 122; impudently challenged, V i 107; 'fac'd it . . . ten', bluffed with a playing-card of only ten spots (proverbial)

FACE (n.), (pun on 'countenance', IV i 85; *see* COUNTENANCE), IV i 87; (v.), brazen, II i 281; Bully, IV iii 124

FAIL, 'fail not . . . cunning', if my cunning and skill do not desert me

FAIN, 'would fain be doing', am eager for action (probably innuendo)

FAIR (adj.), finely dressed, II i 17; (adv.), courteously, civilly, I ii 176; 'fair befall thee', good luck to you; *see* BEARS, IV ii 3

FAIRLY, handsomely, I ii 142

FAITH, (often =) in truth, indeed; 'in faith', in truth

FALCON, i.e. Katherina (Petruchio likens his treatment of Katherina to the methods used to train a bird of prey)

FALL, 'Fall to', begin eating, i.e. partake of

FALL'N OUT, (i) quarrelling, (ii) *see* IV i 48 (quibble)

FAME, reputation

FANCIES, *see* HUMOUR

FANCY (n.), (empty, vain) fantasy, *Induction* i 42; (v.), like, love

FARTHEST, i.e. end of your journey, IV ii 73f.

FARTHINGALES, hooped petticoats

FASHION, design, IV iii 128

FASHIONS, i.e. 'farcy' (a disease consisting of small tumours similar to 'glanders'), III ii 48

FAST, 'fast . . . out', comfortably pass the time in abstinence

FATHER, father-in-law, II i 129, IV v 60

FAULT, 'in the coldest fault', when the scent had been completely lost ('fault' = a break in scent)

FAVOUR, acceptance, permission

FAVOURABLE, *see* STARS

FAY, faith

FEAR, frighten, I ii 207; 'Fear you not him', Don't worry about him; 'fear not me', don't worry about me

FEARS, is frightened of, V ii 16; frightens, V ii 17

FEAST, 'Feast with', Feast on

FEEL, (i) physically feel, (ii) experience, suffer, IV i 55

FEW, 'in a few', to be brief

FIE, For shame (an expression of disgust); 'Fie, fie on', Shame, shame on

FIELD, battlefield, IV v 23

FIGURE, rhetorical device, form, or expression which deviates from normal usage

FIND, *see* BUT, II i 66

FINE, handsomely dressed, II i 309; i.e. fittingly dressed, IV i 120; i.e. consummate (or, perhaps, 'well-dressed'), V i 54

FINGER, *see* PUT, I i 79

FIRE, i.e. make a fire, IV i 32, IV i 39

FIRST, i.e. before me (or 'first of all'), I i 11; 'at the first', *see* KNEW, II i 195

FIT, 'fit the time', fit in with the current fashion

FIVES, swelling at the base of the ear

FLAT, downright

FLATLY, plainly, frankly

FLEET, swift

FLEETER, more swift

FLESH, 'the flesh and the blood', sexual desire

FLORENTIUS' LOVE, (allusion to the story, told by Chaucer in his *The Wife of Bath's Tale* and John Gower in his *Confession Amantis*, of Sir Florent, a knight who is condemned to death unless he can find the answer to a certain riddle. He meets an ugly old hag who promises to tell him the solution on the condition that he in turn promises to marry her. He agrees, she tells him the correct solution and saves his life, and he reluctantly marries her, only to find that she suddenly changes into a young beauty)

FLOURISH, fanfare

FLOURISHETH, prospers

FLOUTS, mocks

FOOL, 'fool, to', harmless weak innocent, compared to, III ii 153

FOOTBOY, page in livery

FOR, (often =) as if; *see* RATHER, *Induction* i 89; because of, I i 1, IV iv 28f.; on account of, I i 88, I ii 121; by, I i 184; *see* HEART, I ii 37; because of, on account of, II i 18; in exchange for, II i 122; With respect to, II i 287; *see* NOTED, III ii 14; in place of, III ii 64; *see*

COMPANY, IV i 161; because of a, IV ii 84; see BETTER, V i 135; 'for so', Because, *Induction* ii 128; 'for the time', for the present; 'am arriv'd for', am on my way to (or 'have arrived in'); 'for why', because, III ii 163; 'For to', To, III ii 243; 'for thee', ready to fight you, IV iii 147

FORBEAR, cease (perhaps Hortensio is holding Bianca's hand in an attempt to teach her the fingering of the lute)

FORBID, forbidden, IV i 155

FORGET HIMSELF, i.e. lose all sense of his real identity

FORGOT, forgotten, III i 2

FORMAL, precise, III i 59

FORSOOTH, in truth, truly

FORSWEAR, abjure, swear to do without, IV ii 26, IV ii 29; see DENY, V i 96

FORSWORN, see WOULD, IV ii 35

FORTH, see MAINTAIN'D, I i 132

FORTHCOMING, ready to appear in court when required

FORTHWITH, immediately

FORTUNE, 'The fouler fortune mine', The worse my luck

FORWARD, presumptuous, II i 73

FORWARD, bold, impudent, III i 1; III i 46; 'myself a forward', myself to be an eager

FOUL, ugly, I ii 67; dirty, IV i 1

FRAME, 'frame your manners . . . time', suit your behaviour to the occasion

FRANTIC, mad

FRENZY, madness

FRESH, radiant, healthy-looking

FRESHER, more radiant, healthy-looking

FRETS, rings of gut tied around the neck and finger-board of a lute, or bars of wood affixed upon it, to regulate the fingering, II i 148; vexations (pun on the above), II i 151

FRETTING, (i) decaying through disuse, (ii) irritable (pun)

FRIENDLY, see MAINTAIN'D, I i 132; i.e. like a friend, IV ii 107

FROLIC, be merry

FROM, see UPON, I ii 179

FROWARD, difficult, refractory, perverse, wilful

FRUITFUL, fertile; fertile (see DUCATS), II i 362

FULL, i.e. fully planned, I i 193

FULL-GORG'D, fully fed

FUME, be in a rage (as in 'fret and fume')

FURNITURE, furnishing, i.e. costume

FUSTIAN, coarse cloth made of cotton and flax

'GAINST, in preparation for

GALLANT, gentleman of fashion

GALLANTS, see GALLANT

GALL'D, scratched, chafed

GALLIASSES, heavy low-built vessels, larger than galleys

GAMBOLD, gambol, frolic

GAMESOME, full of gaiety and sport

GAMESTER, gambler (perhaps an allusion to 'out-vied' of II i 377, or to the fact that Tranio's offer rests on a gamble, not on a certainty)

GAMUT, the diatonic musical scale, III i 65; i.e. learning about the musical scale, III i 69; (perhaps 'the sum total of all that is Hortensio'), III i 70; first note of the musical scale, III i 71

GAWDS, ornaments

GENERALLY, without exception

GENTLE, (often =) noble

GENTLES, gentlemen

GET, beget (pun), II i 402

GIDDY, 'He that is giddy . . . turns round', (proverbial), i.e. people usually attribute their own feelings and preoccupations to others (to whom they may be quite foreign), V ii 20

GIFTS, endowments, qualities

GIRD, taunt, jibe

GIRTH, saddle-strap

GIVE, 'give you over', leave you; 'give him head', (phrase from horsemanship) give him free rein (i.e. cease trying to restrain him); 'give me your hands . . . match', (this may be intended to be a brief ceremony of 'pre-contract' which, according to the customs of Elizabethan England, meant that the couple concerned were officially betrothed); 'give me leave', i.e. allow me to be alone; 'give thanks', say grace

GLANCE, ricochet

GLANDERS, bacterial disease effecting the mouth and nose

GLASS, mirror

GO, see ROUNDLY, IV iv 102; 'Go by, Saint Jeronimy', (a slang phrase of impatient dismissal; perhaps a misquotation from Thomas Kyd's *The Spanish Tragedy*, III xii 31, where the hero Hieronimo warns himself against overhasty action by saying to himself, '*Hieronimo* beware; go by, go by'; Sly confuses Hieronimo with Saint Jerome (or 'Hieronimus' in Latin)); 'go to thy cold bed . . . thee', (probably proverbial); 'Go forward', Carry on, proceed; 'let her go by', leave her alone; 'go to it orderly', proceed in your business properly, with more ceremony; 'go thy ways', go on, carry on (phrase of approval), IV v 23; i.e. well done, carry on, V ii 181; 'It shall go hard if', i.e. It will not be for lack of effort if (and 'it shall be unpleasant if'); 'Go to', come, don't worry (a mild remonstrance), V i 120

GOD-A-MERCY, God have mercy

GOES, 'goes hard', is a serious matter

GOGS-WOUNS, 'by gogs-wouns', by God's wounds (a common oath)

GOOD, see MAKE, IV ii 114

GOODLY, (often =) fine; considerable, *Induction* ii 79; i.e. fine-sounding, II i 255

GOODMAN, husband

GOOD-MORROW, good morning

GOOD-NIGHT, 'good-night our part', farewell to our part of the business

GOODS, see CHATTELS, III ii 226

GRACE, a favour, I ii 128

GRAMERCIES, many thanks (from the Old French 'grant merci')

GRATEFUL, worthy of gratitude

GRATIFY, reward

GREECE, (perhaps an error for 'Greet', a village twenty miles from Stratford)

'GREED, is agreed, II i 262; agreed, II i 289

GREEN, fresh, new, III ii 207; (i) green in colour, (ii) young and fresh, IV v 46

GRIEF, 'the more my grief', and I am all the more sad because of it

GRIEV'D, afflicted

GRISSEL, (allusion to the story of Patient Griselda, told by Boccaccio in his *Decameron*, and Chaucer in his *The Clerk's Tale*, and then by many other writers. Griselda's husband sought to test her patience and obedience by grossly maltreating her. She, however, remained obedient and patient no matter what he did to her)

GROOM, 'a groom indeed', (i) a fine bridegroom (ironic), (ii) a true base menial servingman ('groom')

GROUND, foundation, III i 71

GROW, 'grow into extremes', become excessive

GROWS, will become, *Induction* i 97; 'Whence grows', i.e. what is the reason for

HA', have; 'ha' to thee', i.e. here's to you

HABERDASHER, dealer in or maker of hats and other articles of clothing

HABILIMENTS, clothes

HABIT, clothing, apparel, II i 38 *Stage Direction*, IV iii 170; costume, III ii 96; manner, appearance, V i 62

HABITS, garments

HAD, see LIEF, I i 128; 'had you need', you need to

HADST THOU, if you had

HAGGARD, intractable wild hawk, IV i 177; (i.e., here, 'light woman'), IV ii 39

HAL'D, dragged about

HALF, 'I'll be your half', I'll share the wager with you (i.e. split the bet and the profits)

HALF-CHEEK'D BIT, bit on which the 'cheeks' (rings attaching the bit to the bridle) (or only one of the 'cheeks') had become broken (which therefore made it difficult to control the horse)

HALT, limp; (pun on 'come' = walk), III ii 85

HALVES, sharers in my wager

HAND, see SEE, I ii 143; see AT, IV i 102; 'at any hand', in any case; 'on either hand', i.e. by both parties to the agreement

HANGINGS, draperies with which beds and walls were hung

HANGS, see THEREBY

HAP, 'whose hap shall be', whoever it is whose good fortune it shall be; 'Hap what hap may', Whatever may happen

HAPLY, Perhaps; perhaps (or 'auspiciously'), I i 8; with luck, fortunately, I ii 54

HAPPILY, propitiously, I ii 209; fortunately, IV iv 19; haply, perchance, IV iv 54

HAPPY, see IN, *Induction* i 128; 'Happy man . . . dole', (proverbial) May the lot (of the successful suitor) be to be a happy man

HARD, see GOES, IV ii 80; see GO, IV iv 103; 'hard of hearing', (pun on 'heard', which was pronounced in the same way as 'hard'; see SOMETHING)

HARSH, rough, III ii 101

HAS, he has, IV iv 77

HASTY-WITTED BODY, quick-witted person

HA'T, i.e. receive the money you have won in the bet, V ii 181

HAVE, 'have to't afresh', we will renew our battle; 'I'll have them', I wish them to be, i.e. see that they are; 'Have to', Let me go to, try to win, IV v 77; 'Have at you', I shall attack you, V ii 45

HAVING, 'having come', i.e. I, having come

HE, person, III ii 230; 'he of both', whichever of you two

HEAD, see GIVE, I ii 245

HEAD-STALL, part of the bridle over the horse's head

HEARING, 'a good hearing', a pleasant thing to hear; 'harsh hearing', unpleasant thing to hear

HEARKEN, i.e. lie in wait

HEARK'NING STILL, always listening

HEART, 'for my heart', i.e. for my life

HEAVY, 'heavy chance', sad happening; 'as heavy as my weight should be', i.e. I am as good a woman as I should be with as good a reputation as I should have (perhaps an allusion to the fact that counterfeit coins tended to weigh less than good current coins)

HEEDLESS, careless

HELP, 'help me to', (i) help me find, (ii) help me become (private jest on Hortensio's part)

HENCE, go hence, III ii 193, IV iii 178

HER, herself, IV iv 63; 'her . . . her . . .', i.e. Bianca . . . Katherina's . . ., I i 89

HERALD, expert on heraldry

HERCULES, (a mythological Greek hero, son of Zeus and Alcmena, who possessed fabulous strength. He married Megara, daughter of the King of Thebes, but was driven insane by Zeus's wife Hera (who was jealous of her husband's relationship with Alcmena) and killed Megara and all his children by her. When he returned to his senses, he went into exile and bound himself to serve Eurystheus, king of Mycenae, for twelve years, during which time he performed his twelve 'Labours': he killed the Nemean Lion and the Hydra, captured the Erymanthian Boar and the Hind of Artemis; he killed the man-eating Stymphalian birds, cleansed the Augean Stables, captured the Cretan Bull, the horses of Diomedes, and the girdle of Hippolyta; he killed the monster Geryon, captured Cerberus, and finally stole the apples of the Hesperides)

HIC IBAT . . . SENIS, Here ran the (river) Simois; here is the Sigeian land (Troy); here stood the lofty towers of old Priam (the King of Troy; these lines come from the *Heroides* i 33–34, a poem by the Latin poet Ovid)

HID, hidden

HIE, 'hie you', hurry

HIGH-CROSS, cross set on a pedestal in a market-place

HILDING, base wretch

HIM, (often =) himself; i.e. him for, III ii 172

HIPP'D, lamed in the hip

HISTORY, narrative

HIT, i.e. defined exactly, II i 197

HITS YOU, strikes you a bitter blow

HOLD (n.), (his) keeping (perhaps 'fortified place'), I ii 116; (v.) retain, keep, I i 106; wager, III ii 79; see BAY, V ii 56; 'hold with her', stand up to her handling, II i 145; 'hold thee . . . drink', i.e. Tranio gives him a tip; 'hold your own', play your part well

HOLIDAME, 'by my holidame', by all that I hold sacred ('holidame' originally = 'halidom', i.e. 'holiness', but later came to be interpreted as a reference to the Blessed Virgin Mary)

HONOURABEL, becoming, decorous

HOP ME, hop (for me)

HOPE (n.), 'in hope to speed alone', hoping to be the sole winner ('speed' = succeed); 'hope' (v.), hope for, expect, V ii 85

HORN, (i) allusion to the horn or horns which were jocularly supposed to grow on the foreheads of cuckolds, (ii) (innuendo, i.e. = phallus), IV i 24; 'your head and butt . . . horn', your butting head was a horned head (allusion to a cuckold's 'horns'; see *above*)

HORSE, horses (a common old form of the plural), III ii 200

HORSE-TAIL, horse's tail

HOT, violent, hot-tempered, II i 286; see POT, IV i 5; angry, violent, IV i 17; i.e. likely to be productive of choler, IV iii 25; 'hot office', i.e. duty of making the fire

HOURS, see APPOINTED HOURS, I i 103

HOUSE, i.e. tavern, *Induction* ii 84, *Induction* ii 88f.; see CHATTELS, III ii 226

HOUSEHOLD, domestic, II i 270; 'household stuff', household furnishings (Sly perhaps misunderstands 'stuff' of *Induction* ii 136 as meaning 'furnishings'; he may, however, mean 'domestic goings-on')

HOW, (expression of surprise, i.e. 'Really!'), V ii 82; 'How now', Hello, how are you, what are you doing; how are you, what are you saying, IV v 41; what are you saying, V i 30; What is all this, V i 60; 'How but well', It could be nothing other than good success; 'how you can', however you may, III ii 199

HUMBLE (v.), see DAUGHTER OF AGENOR, I i 164

HUMOUR, mood, whim, I ii 105; (ill-balanced) disposition, III ii 29; caprice, whim, III ii 68; see KILLS, IV i 164; 'idle humour', vain, foolish fancy, aberration of mind; 'the humour . . . fancies', i.e. some

99

ornament of a very fanciful design (in place of a feather)

HUNGERLY, sparsely

HURLY, disturbance

HUSBAND, 'good husband', careful manager

HUSBANDED, 'husbanded with modesty', carried out with moderation

HUSHT, Keep quiet

IDLE, vain, foolish, *Induction* ii 12; foolish, meaningless, *Induction* ii 81

IDLENESS, *see* LOVE

I'FAITH, In truth, indeed

ILL-FAVOUR'D, endowed with bad qualities (perhaps not, here, 'ugly')

ILL-SEEMING, unpleasant to look at

IMAGE, likeness (allusion to the ancient opinion that sleep was the image of death)

IMPATIENT, angry, *Induction* i 97

IMPORT, *see* OCCASION

IMPRIMIS, (Latin) first, to begin with

IN, go in, *Induction* i 134, V i 120, V i 125; *see* PERIL, *Induction* ii 120; *see* 'TIS, II i 398; *see* PARTS, III i 58; 'in happy time', opportunely; 'in all suits', in every respect (pun on 'suits' = articles of clothing); 'in a few', to be brief; 'in place', present, I ii 153; 'in possession', i.e. in immediate possession, II i 121; 'in good time', indeed, forsooth, II i 194; 'In resolution', Resolved to hold true to the intention I mentioned before (*see* IV ii 28ff.); 'in that', because, IV iii 83

INDIFFERENT, equally, I ii 177; 'indifferent knit', normal, unostentatious pattern, texture

INFUSED WITH, inspired, i.e. dominated, by

INGENIOUS, intellectual

INGRATE, 'be ingrate', be ungrateful

INSTITUTE, begin

INSTRUMENT, i.e. the lute, II i 98

INSTRUMENTS, musical instruments, I i 82

INTEND, pretend, assert, IV i 187

INTENT, purpose

INTO, *see* DECLINING, *Induction* i 117

INTOLERABLE, intolerably, I ii 87

INVENTIONS, 'Both our inventions . . . one', Both of our schemes agree and concur as one; 'odd inventions', strange and perverse new ideas

IO, (allusion to the myth, related by Ovid the Latin poet in his *Metamorphoses* i 588–600, that Jupiter, the King of the Roman gods, fell in love with Io, the daughter of the river god Inachus, and pursued her when she fled his advances. In a vain attempt to conceal his activities from his wife Juno, Jupiter shrouded Io in a dense mist under the cover of which he raped her and then changed her into a cow)

IS, i.e. is indeed mad at the present time, *Induction* i 62; i.e. are, III ii 147; are ('all things' is thought of as a collective noun), IV i 101

IT, i.e. marriage, I i 62; 'it is best', *see* PUT, I i 78; 'It was the friar . . . way –', (fragment of an old ballad)

I'TH', in the

IWIS, certainly

JACK, knave, rogue; 'Jack boy! ho, boy!', (an allusion to a catch-song, the first words of which are: 'Jack boy, ho boy, News:/The cat is in the well . . .')

JACKS, (i) man-servants, (ii) drinking-vessels

JADE, ill-conditioned horse (of either sex) which soon tires

JADES, worthless, worn-out horses

JAMY, *see* SAINT JAMY

JARS, is out of tune, III i 38; i.e. annoys him (pun on III i 38), III i 45

JAY, a bird whose plumage is bright but whose song is harsh and chattering

JEALOUS, suspicious

JERKIN, short jacket

JERONIMY, *see* GO

JILLS, (i) maid-servants, (ii) small drinking-vessels

JOGGING, 'You may be jogging . . . green', i.e. you can get an early start (proverbial expression used for suggesting the departure of unwelcome guests: *see* GREEN)

JOIN'D-STOOL, stool made by a joiner (term of disparagement; *see* MOVEABLE)

JOINTURE, marriage settlement

JOLLY, overbearing

JOLTHEADS, blockheads

JOT, 'not a jot of', never mention the name of ('jot' = small particle)

JOVE, Jupiter (*see* DAUGHTER OF AGENOR)

JUMP, *see* INVENTIONS

JUNKETS, sweetmeats

KATE HALL, (perhaps an allusion to a place of that name; 'Kate of Kate Hall' may be meant to imply that she is so remarkable that the place in which she lives takes its name from her rather than her family or father)

KATED, i.e. afflicted with the Katherina-disease (which is synonymous with being 'mated'; pun on 'mated'; *see* MATED)

KEEP (n.), keeping, custody (perhaps 'fortified place'), I ii 115; (v.), i.e. keep silent, I i 204; 'Keep house', i.e. Entertain in the appropriate style; 'Keep you warm', (allusion to the proverb 'He is wise enough that can keep himself warm (i.e. keep himself out of the rain)', (Katherina implies that Petruchio has only the minimum intelligence necessary to enable him to be able to survive)

KEEP'ST, *see* WHOM

KENNEL, gutter, surface drain of a street

KERSEY, coarse woollen cloth

KILL, 'kill a wife with kindness', (ironical allusion to the proverbial expression used to describe the harming of someone by treating them with excessive kindness)

KILLS, 'kills her . . . humour', overmasters her by outdoing her in her own unbalanced disposition

KINDLY, i.e. welcome, *Induction* i 11; naturally, convincingly, *Induction* i 64; 'kindly beholding', naturally indebted

KINDNESS, i.e. feelings proper to kinship, V ii 5; i.e. natural benevolence, V ii 13

KINDRED, 'of no kindred', i.e. which do not match

KISS, 'kiss their hands', (to kiss one's own hand was a sign of respect)

KISS'D, i.e. knelt upon, I i 165

KITES, small hawks

KNACK, knicknack, trifle

KNAVE, scoundrel, *Induction* ii 21

KNAVE'S, scoundrel's, I ii 12

KNAV'RY, 'all this knav'ry', i.e. all such tricks

KNEW, 'I knew you at the first', I recognised at the very first that

KNOCK, (i.e. for admittance; Grumio takes the word to mean merely 'strike'), I ii 5ff.; 'I should knock . . . worst', i.e. You make me strike you so that you can have an excuse for striking me even more severely afterwards

KNOW, think, IV iv 48; 'I know him well', i.e. His name is well known to me, II i 70

LAMPASS, thick growth of skin over the upper teeth of a horse's mouth making it almost impossible for it to eat

LARGESS, liberal gifts

'LARUMS, alarums, (*see* ALARUMS)

LATE, recently, IV i 124; *see* BETTER, V i 135

LATIN, (i.e. Grumio has not understood the Italian), I ii 28

LAVE, wash

LAW, 'by law', in court, with judicial proceedings, *Induction* i 10

LAY, blame, IV iii 177; 'lay their heads', i.e. plot

LAYING, betting

LEAD, 'lead apes in hell', (proverbial occupation of old maids; they were supposed to 'lead apes in hell' because they had no children of their own to lead to heaven)

LEASES, stretches of pasture land

LEAVE (n.), *see* GIVE, III i 57; permission, IV iii 73; 'give me leave', (perhaps) leave me alone (or 'excuse me'), II i 46; 'leave' (v.), cease from (*see* TUNE), III i 24; 'To leave frivolous circumstances', To have done with pointless and frivolous matters

LECTURE, lesson; *see* TUNE, III i 23

LECTURES, *see* READ

LEDA'S DAUGHTER, Helen of Troy (perhaps an allusion to Marlowe's famous line (*Doctor Faustus* scene xiii 91); 'Was this the face that launched a thousand ships?')

LEET, manorial court (where complaints about short measure would be heard)

LEFT, 'left we', did we break off our lesson

'LEGES, alleges

LEISURE, *see* STAYS, IV iii 59; 'stay . . . leisure', i.e. wait until I am ready

LET, i.e. provided that, II i 379; 'let me alone', leave me alone, i.e. rely on me; 'let't alone', i.e. do nothing more about the matter

LEWD, worthless

LIE, lodge, IV iv 56

LIEF, 'had as lief', would as willingly

LIES, 'The note lies in's throat', i.e. (i) The note is an out-and-out liar, (ii) (perhaps) The musical note is in his throat (i.e. the words come from his mouth and are only an assertion unsupported by any evidence)

LIGHT (adj.), (i) slight, delicate, (ii) wanton, (iii) (in music) having no 'burden' (= groundbass; *see* BURDEN), II i 202; quick, elusive, II i 203; (v.), 'lighton', happen upon, find, I i 109, I i 125

LIGHTED, chanced

LIGHTNESS, wantonness

LIKE (adj.), same, IV ii 32; similar (in appearance), IV ii 105; i.e. as properly befits, IV iv 44; 'the like', a similar, II i 77; (adv.), (often =) likely; probable that, III ii 209; (v.), i.e. approve of, IV iv 32; *see* AN, IV iv 55; 'like not of', do not approve of

LIKES, pleases, IV iv 62

LINK, blacking (made out of burnt torches ('= links'), or, perhaps, the smoke of torches) used to colour old hats

LIST (n.), strip of cloth, III ii 63; (v.), listen, II i 355; see SEIZE, III i 89; chooses, cares to, III ii 161; please, choose, IV v 7

LIST'NING, you to listen

LIVE, see WILL, I ii 193

LIVELY, realistically

LOGGER-HEADED, blockheaded, stupid

LONG, after a long time, V ii 1

'LONGETH, belongs, IV ii 45; ''longeth to', belongeth to, i.e. befits, IV iv 7

LONGLY, persistently, for (such) a long time

LOOK, long, hope, IV iv 92; 'look unto', take care of; 'Look that', Take care that, IV ii 108; 'Look what', Whatever, IV iii 188

LOOK'D FOR, expected

LOOSE-BODIED GOWN, loosely-fitting dress (often worn by prostitutes, among others)

LOSE, 'lose your arms', lose your right to a coat of arms (the sign of a gentleman; or, perhaps, if Petruchio has taken hold of Katherina, 'relax your hold on me')

LOVE, i.e. a love-suit, I ii 133; 'love in idleness', (quibble on (i) the proverb 'Idleness begets love', (ii) 'Love-in-Idleness', the popular name for the pansy)

LOVELY, loving, III ii 119

LOWLY, humble, Induction i 112

LUCENTIO, 'Lucentio is your name', (presumably Baptista learns this from an inscription in the books)

LUCRECE, Lucretia (a legendary Roman woman, wife of Tarquinius Lucretius, who committed suicide after she had been raped by Sextus Tarquinius. Shakespeare tells her story in his The Rape of Lucrece)

LUNATIC, (adj.), mad

LURE, see STOOP

LUSTY, lively, vigorous, spirited

LYING'ST, most untruthful

MADE, 'made it good', i.e. put matters right (by picking up the scent)

MAID, see WOMAN'S MAID, Induction ii 88

MAINTAIN'D, 'it shall be . . . maintain'd till', i.e. we shall agree to remain friendly just until

MAKE, i.e. became, I i 241, I ii 242; 'make way', go; 'Make it no wonder', Don't be surprised; 'make the matter good', i.e. put the plan into effect; 'make your best of it', make the best you can of it

MALT-HORSE DRUDGE, slow, heavy horse used to work a treadmill to grind malt

MAN (n.), servant, I i 0 Stage Direction; (v.), tame, IV i 177

MANNERS, behaviour, I i 236

MAR, 'mar it to the time', ruin it for all time (quibble on 'to the time' = exactly in accordance with contemporary fashion)

MARIAN HACKET, (perhaps an allusion to the Hacket family which seems to have lived in the parish of Quinton, in which part of the hamlet of Wincot, four miles south of Stratford, lay)

MARK, watch attentively, I i 247 Stage Direction, IV ii 5

MARK'D, noticed

MARKS, (a 'mark' was a sum worth thirteen shillings and fourpence), V ii 35

MARRY, Indeed (originally an oath: 'By (the Blessed Virgin) Mary')

MART, 'desperate mart', a bargain ('mart') desperately made (i.e. of doubtful success)

MARVEL, ''Tis marvel', It's strange (i.e. that you are unaware of this)

MARVELLOUS, marvellously

MASQUING STUFF, i.e. material fit only for a 'masque' (an amateur theatrical entertainment in which strange and exotic costumes were often worn)

MASTER, i.e. Tranio (see IV iv 59), IV iv 75

MATCH, see GIVE, II i 311; 'A match', agreed, it's a bet, V ii 74

MATED, 'madly mated', (i) matched in marriage with a madman, (ii) checkmated ('mated') by an opponent who is her equal in madness, (iii) madly stupefied

MATES, rude fellows, I i 58; (i) rude fellows, (ii) husbands (pun), I i 59; i.e. ship-mates (see ABROAD), III ii 167

MATTER, subject, story, I i 243

MAZE, uncertain course (i.e. travelling or looking for a wife)

ME, (i.e. 'for me', but Grumio misunderstands), I ii 8ff.

MEACOCK, timid, spiritless

MEADS, meadows

MEAN, of low rank (i.e. dressed as a schoolmaster), II i 38 Stage Direction; poor (in quality), IV iii 166; poor, IV iii 176; petty, contemptible (with a pun following); 'mean, indeed, respecting you', moderate (in temper) compared with you

MEANER, i.e. poorer (than I really am)

MEANEST, lowliest

MEANS, plans, V i 32
MEASURE, *see* CAROUSE, III ii 221
MEASURES, judges
MEAT, food in general, IV iii 9; food, IV iii 40
MEDDLE NOT WITH, have nothing to do with
MEET, proper, fitting, *Induction* ii 128, V ii 141
MEMORY, 'of worthy memory', worthy of remembrance
MEND, improve, add to, I ii 147; improve, i.e. make a better job of, IV i 131
MENDED, improved, put right, IV i 160; rectified, V ii 25
MERCATANTE, merchant (Italian)
MEREST, *see* CRIED
MESS, dish
METE-YARD, measuring stick a yard long
METHINKS, it seems to me
MEW, shut, cage (a term from falconry used to describe the caging of a falcon)
MEW'D, *see* MEW
MI PERDONATO, pardon me (Italian)
MIGHTY, illustrious, important, II i 103
MILCH-KINE . . . PAIL, dairy cattle
MIND (n.), opinion, I i 21; intention, I ii 75; (v.), pay attention, I i 242
MINERVA, (the Roman goddess of wisdom and the patroness of the arts and trades)
MINION, impudent, spoiled hussy
MISUSE, i.e. abuse
MODESTIES, i.e. ability to control yourselves
MODESTY, *see* HUSBANDED, *Induction* i 66
MONEY, *see* ENOUGH, I i 127
MONUMENT, portent
MORALIZE, interpret
MORE, again, in the future, IV ii 29; *see* WRONG, IV iii 2
MORROW, morning
MOSE IN THE CHINE, suffer from a dark discharge from the nostrils (characteristic of 'glanders')
MOTHER WIT, natural, innate intelligence
MOTION, proposal
MOULD, i.e. nature
MOV'D, impelled, II i 193; annoyed, angered, V ii 142
MOVEABLE, (i) person, thing, subject to movement, change, (ii) a piece of movable furniture (pun)
MOVES, disturbs, troubles
MUM, silence, keep silent
MUSCADEL, sweet wine (*see* WINE)
MUST, must come, III ii 223; 'must I', must I go, V i 9

MYSELF, (often =) I myself; 'myself, that', I myself, who

NAIL, (unit of measure of cloth length, the equivalent of one sixteenth of a yard)
NAILS, *see* BLOW
NAME, *see* VERY, IV iii 32
NAPKIN, handkerchief
NARROWLY, attentively
NARROW-PRYING, over-inquisitive
NATURALLY, i.e. realistically
NEAR, nearly, IV iv 4
NEAR-LEGG'D BEFORE, with knock-kneed forelegs
NEAT'S FOOT, the foot of an ox
NEEDS, of necessity
NE'ER A WHIT, Not in the least
NEVER, *see* TUNE, III i 25; *see* BETTER, V i 135
NICE, capricious (or, perhaps, 'foolish')
NILL, 'will you, nill you', whether you like it or not
NIT, egg of a louse
NO, 'No shame but mine', No one other than myself is shamed; 'say no', i.e. disapprove, III ii 137
NOD, begin to fall asleep, IV i 190
NODDLE, head
NONE, have nothing to do with, IV iii 100; 'none so . . . thirsty', no one, no matter how tired or thirsty they may be
NOTE, (probably 'memorandum from the supposed schoolmaster about books for Bianca'), I ii 141
NOTED, 'to be noted for', in order to get a reputation for being
NOUGHT, 'nought remains but so', there is nothing left to be done but this
NOURISHETH, (probably) provides the good things of life
NOW, 'now to weep', for weeping now
NURSE, nourisher
NURSERY OF ARTS, *see* PADUA

O', On, I ii 105
OATS, 'the oats . . . horses', i.e. the horses have had more oats than they could eat
OBEISANCE, 'do him obeisance', i.e. show him all respect due to a social superior
OBLIVION, i.e. forgetfulness
OCCASION, 'occasion of', an opportunity for, II i 36; 'occasion of import', important reason
ODDS, advantage (perhaps with a quibble on 'odds' = pieces of cloth left over after the

making of a garment which the tailor could claim for himself)

O'ER-RUN, flowed over

OF, during, *Induction* ii 80; on, IV i 60, V ii 72; from, IV i 91, IV iii 28; *see* OURSELVES, IV i 158

OFFER, present, introduce, I ii 129; presume, dare, V i 52; declare, V ii 162

OFFICE, duty, *Induction* i 71; *see* HOT, IV i 28, IV i 31; function, job, V ii 36

OFFICER, constable, arresting-officer, V i 81; i.e. one who does his duty, V ii 37; servant, IV i 42

OLD, rare, III ii 30

ON, about, IV i 26; 'on the score', in debt (a 'score' was originally an account kept by cutting notches in a stick)

ONCE, *see* BETTER, V i 135

ONE, i.e. person, *Induction* i 57; (quibble on III ii 77), III ii 81; *see* AND, IV ii 101; *see* CONSENT, IV iv 35

OPPOS'D ... HEART, even though it is against my heartfelt desire

OR, 'Or ere', Before

ORCHARD, (probably) garden

ORDER, method, III i 63; 'this order', these measures

ORDERLY, properly

ORDERS, 'orders grey', i.e. the 'friar' was a 'Grey' or 'Franciscan' Friar

ORDNANCE, cannon

OTHER MORE, other people besides, I ii 118

OUR, my (Christopher Sly adopts the 'royal' plural), *Induction* ii 72

OURSELVES, 'of ourselves, ourselves are', by our nature we are already

OUT, (expression of anger), IV i 130; 'out before', i.e. on the forestage (or 'proceeds the others on to the stage'); 'Out of hope of all but', Hoping for nothing except

OUT-VIED, out-bidded (used of a card-player who refuses to stake any more on his hand; to 'vie' = to place a stake at cards)

OVERBLOWN, that have blown over

OVER-EYING OF, observing

OVERLEATHER, leather upper

OVER-REACH, outmanoeuvre, get the better of

OVID, Publius Ovidius Naso (*c.* 43 BC–17 AD, the Latin poet, author of the *Amores* (sophisticated love-elegies), the *Heroides* (dramatic monologues in the form of love-letters between mythological lovers), *Ars Amatoria* (*The Art of Love*), and *Metamorphoses*)

OX, *see* CHATTELS

OYSTER, *see* APPLE

PACK, be gone, II i 176

PACKING, conspiracy, plotting

PACK-THREAD, string

PADUA, (Padua's university, founded in the thirteenth century, was famous throughout Europe as a centre of learning)

PAGE, youth employed as a servant or attendant

PAIN, *see* USUAL PAIN

PAINS, labour, trouble

PAINT, i.e. redden with scratches

PANTALOON, foolish old man (a stock character in Italian comedy, where he was invariably clad in tights, a red jacket, a long black sleeved gown, and black slippers), I i 45 *Stage Direction*; i.e. Gremio, III i 35

PAPER, i.e. the 'note' of, I ii 141

PARIS, (a Trojan prince who was the son of Priam, King of Troy, and who stole Helen of Troy from her husband Menelaus)

PARK, country-house grounds

PARLE, *see* BROOK'D PARLE

PART, 'part the fray', separate the fighters, stop the brawl

PART'S, party's (*see* AFFIED), IV iv 50

PARTS, 'in three parts', for three voices

PASS (n.), situation, V ii 124; (v.), goes beyond, I i 123; settle upon, IV iv 45; transact, IV iv 57; 'pass assurance', give a guarantee

PASSING, surpassingly, extremely, exceedingly; to be exceedingly, III ii 24

PASSION, 'merry passion', fit of laughter

PATE, head

PAUCAS PALLABRIS, few words (from the Spanish 'pocas palabras'; this may be an allusion to Thomas Kyd's *The Spanish Tragedy* III xiv 118 where the hero Hieronimo uses the phrase to caution himself against revealing too much of what he knows; *see* GO)

PEASANT SWAIN, lowly, rascally country bumpkin

PEAT, pet, spoiled darling

PEDANT, schoolmaster, IV ii 63, IV ii 71 *Stage Direction*

PEDASCULE, little pedant (a specially-coined word consisting of a pseudo-Latin diminutive with a vocative ending)

PEERETH, appears

PEEVISH, obstinate, wilful

PEGASUS, (i.e. an inn called 'The Pegasus'

after the winged horses of the same name in classical mythology)

PEREMPTORY, resolved, resolute

PERIL, 'In peril to incur', On peril of your incurring

PHEEZE, 'I'll pheeze you', (vague threat) I'll fix you, I'll do for you ('pheeze' originally = drive away, frighten off)

PIE, meat-pie

PIECED, mended, III ii 54; joined, III ii 56

PIERCING, moving

PILLORY, instrument of punishment made of movable boards through which a prisoner's legs, arms, or head could be thrust and in which they could be kept immobile to leave the prisoner prey to popular ridicule

PINCH'D, i.e. discomforted

PIP, 'a pip out', see TWO

PITCHERS, 'Pitchers have ears', i.e. there may be listeners (proverbial saying punning on 'ears' = (i) handles for pitchers, (ii) organs of hearing)

PITH, 'the pith of all', the crux of the matter

PITHY, condensed

PITTANCE, scanty meal

PLACE, 'in place', present, I ii 153

PLAINNESS, frankness, I i 147

PLANTETH, implants (in a human-being)

PLASH, pool, puddle

PLATE, utensils of silver

PLEASANT, (often =) merry

PLEASE, 'Please ye', May it please you that; 'please it you that I', Do you wish me to

PLEASURE, will, command, I i 81; wish, I i 206

PLEDGE, surety

PLY, work with, II i 25; 'ply his book', study

'POINT, appoint

'POINTED, appointed

POINTS, tagged laces used for tying the hose

POLICY, a deliberate crafty purpose

POLITICLY, shrewdly, in a crafty way

POOREST, most insignificant

PORRINGER, small basin from which soup, porridge, etc., would be eaten

PORT, state, (high) style of living, I i 198; 'bearing my port', taking on himself my style, demeanour

PORTION, estate

POT, 'were I not a little pot . . . hot', (proverbial phrase used to describe a person with a quick temper)

PRACTICE, instruction, II i 163

PRACTISE ON, play a trick upon

PRATING, foolish prattling (see THINK)

PRAY'D, (perhaps 'pleaded')

PREFER, recommend

PREFERMENT, giving of precedence in marriage to

PREPOSTEROUS ASS, idiot who inverts the natural order of things ('preposterous' is used in its literal (Latin) sense, i.e. one who puts later things ('post-') first ('pre-'))

PREROGATIVE, precedence

PRESENT (adj.), immediate, IV iii 5, IV iii 14; (v.), bring a legal charge against, Induction ii 85

PRESENTERS, i.e. those who, by means of a prologue or commentary, introduce or present a play to the spectators

PRESENTLY, immediately

PREVENTED, forestalled

PRICK'D IN'T, pinned on to it

PRICKS, that spurs, incites

PRITHEE, (I) beg you

PROCEEDERS, (pun on the term 'proceed' = to advance in a university course from graduation as a BA to some higher degree, e.g. MA; cp. 'Master of your art', IV ii 9)

PROCURE ME, procure for me

PRODIGY, marvel, omen

PROFIT YOU IN, i.e. do you make good progress in, benefit from

PROMISE, assure, II i 177

PROOF, see SORTED, IV iii 43; 'to the proof', in tested ('proved') steel armour (or 'so as to be invulnerable'; 'proof' = armour tested and proved to be impenetrable)

PROPER, 'proper stripling', fine and handsome young man (ironic)

PROUD, (perhaps) stuffed out with money, IV iii 167

PROVE, (often =) turn out to be; 'prove a soldier', (i) become a soldier, (ii) put a soldier to the test (pun); 'prove upon thee', establish by fighting you

PUMPS, light shoes, slippers for indoor use

PUT, 'it is best Put finger . . . eye', i.e. the best thing she can do is to weep if she knew of a good reason for doing so ('Put . . . eye' is proverbial); 'put me in heart', encouraged; 'put her down', (i) get the better of her, (ii) have sexual relations with her (so Hortensio puns, V ii 36)

QUAFF, drink off

QUAFF'D OFF, drank back all of (see WINE)

QUAINT, cunning, clever, III ii 143; elegant, well-made, IV iii 102
QUALIFIED, 'so qualified', of such qualities
QUANTITY, fragment
QUARTS, see SEAL'D QUARTS
QUEEN OF CARTHAGE, see ANNA
QUICKEN, stimulate, enliven
QUIET, 'quiet in the match', peace and quiet as a result of a good marriage for Katherina
QUIT, 'be quit with', get even with
QUOTH, said

RAIL, scold (see ROPE-TRICKS), I ii 109; 'rail upon', chide, loudly criticise, Induction ii 84
RAILS, chides
RANGING, (i) straying (of a hawk), (ii) inconstant (in love)
RASCAL, base, good-for-nothing, II i 156
RATED, i.e. capable of being driven away from (by being scolded)
RATES, scolds
RATHER, 'The rather for', All the more so because
RAY'D, dirtied
RAYED . . . YELLOWS, defiled with jaundice
RE, i.e. the second note of the musical scale
READ, study, IV ii 6; 'read . . . lectures', teach no other subjects
READIEST, easiest, most direct
REASON, see SEE, II i 399
REBUS'D, (blunder for 'abused')
RECK'NING, account
RECKON'D UP, mentioned, enumerated
REDIME . . . MINIMO, ransom yourself from captivity as cheaply as you can (words from the Latin author Terence's Eunuchus I i 29, quoted here in the form which they take in the Elizabethan Latin Grammar by Lily)
REGARD, dutiful attendance, IV i 110
REHEARS'D, recounted
REMEMB'RED, 'be remb'red', recollect, IV iii 96
REMOVES, 'or not removes . . . edge in me', or, at least, cannot blunt the keenness ('edge') of my desire ('affection') (to marry you)
REPAIR, 'repair . . . wear in me', change for the better what she will receive when she takes me as her husband ('wear' may mean 'wear away', i.e. an innuendo)
REPAST, food
REPOSE (v.), rest
REPUTE, consider
RESOLUTION, see IN

RESOLVE, IV ii 7
RESPECTING, see MEAN (adj.)
REST, remain, I ii 270; 'let the mustard rest', i.e. don't bother with the mustard
RESTRAINED, pulled back
RESTS, remains to be done
RETURN, i.e. go, IV i 73
REVEL IT, revel
REVERENCE, obeisance
RHEIMS, (a university was founded at Rheims in France in 1547)
RICHARD CONQUEROR, (i.e. a blunder for 'William the Conqueror')
RIGHT (adj.), true, real, IV iv 12; proper, V ii 109; (n.), act of justice, I ii 235
RING (n.), i.e. prize (proberbial allusion to the jousting-game in which contestants tried to pierce and carry off a ring on a post by running or riding at it with a lance; see I i 136ff.), I i 135; (v.), (pun on 'wring'), I ii 17
RIVAL, 'the rival of my love', my rival in love (i.e. Gremio)
ROAD, 'Marseilles road', sheltered anchorage of Marseilles
ROPE-TRICKS, (precise meaning unknown; perhaps (i) a blunder for 'rhetoric'; (or) (ii) Grumio's version of 'rope-tricks' (a word used by Thomas Nashe in his Have with You to Saffron-Walden (published in 1596) which probably means 'rhetoric which is so outrageously bombastic that its author deserves to be hanged'); (or) (iii) rascally conduct which deserves to be punished with hanging; (or) (iv) bawdy innuendo)
ROUNDLY, see COME, I ii 57; see TAKE, III ii 210; frankly, plainly, V ii 21; 'I'll roundly go about her', I'll approach her openly and directly (with a view to asking her to marry me)
ROUT, crowd (of guests)
RUDESBY, unmannerly, rude fellow
RUFFLING, gay, swaggering
RUFFS, stiffly starched fluted and wheel-shaped collars
RUN, run-up (i.e. to get up speed for a slide), IV i 13
RUSH-CANDLE, feeble candle made by dipping a rush into grease
RUSHES, used as floor-coverings

SACK, Spanish white wine, Induction ii 2
SADNESS, 'in good sadness', in sober earnestness
SAFE, i.e. safely taken care of, IV iv 80

SAINT JAMY, (perhaps an allusion to James the Greater or James the less (two of Christ's disciples) or to James, the first Bishop of Jerusalem and brother of Jesus, who was supposed to have written *The General Epistle of James*)

SATIETY, overfeeding

SATISFY YOU IN, convince you of

SAVING, With all respect for

SAY, 'say no', i.e. disapprove, III ii 137

SCANT, diminish (*see* EXCESS), III ii 112

SCAPE, escape

SCAPES, escapes

SCHOOL'D, instructed in the part he has to play

SCIENCES, branches of learning

SCORE (n.), *see* ON, *Induction* ii 21; (v.), reckon, put me on the record as, *Induction* ii 21

SCORN, scorns (agreeing with 'I' of IV ii 17)

SCRIVENER, notary (a clerk authorised to draw up contracts)

SEAL, ratify (as one would ratify a legal document by affixing a waxen seal to it)

SEAL'D QUARTS, quart jugs stamped with an official mark to show that they hold the correct quantity

SECRET, intimate, in my confidence

SEDGES, grasslike plants growing in marshy places

SEE, 'see that at any hand', make sure of that in any case; 'I see no reason but', I see that there is nothing else to be done other than that

SEEN, *see* WELL SEEN, I ii 131

SEIZE, 'seize thee that list', Let whoever wishes to catch you

SEMIRAMIS, legendary queen of Assyria, notorious for her voluptuousness and sensuality

SENSELESS, idiotic, unreasonable

SENSIBLE, (i) capable of being felt with the senses, (ii) capable of being understood, (iii) rational (pun), IV i 56; judicious, discriminating, V ii 18

SERMON, 'Making a sermon . . . her', Giving her a lecture on the virtues of moderation and restraint

SERVE, *see* BECOME, I i 15; 'serve in', serve up (like a dish), III i 14; 'Will serve the turn', Who will do for our purpose

SERVICEABLE, diligent in serving

SESSA, (meaning uncertain; perhaps 'let it go', or, 'be off with you')

SET, 'Set foot under your table', i.e. Become your dependant; 'Set your countenance', Put on a grave expression

SEVERALLY, in different ways, by different doors at the back of the stage, II i 316 *Stage Direction*; separately, one by one, (or) by different doors, IV i 162 *Stage Direction*

SEXTON, bell-ringer and grave-digger

SHAKE, shake to pieces, shake off

SHARP, hungry

SHEATHING, having a sheath made for it

SHEEP'S LEATHER, i.e. leather of inferior quality (pigskin was usually used to make fine saddlery)

SHIFT (n.), (perhaps) expedient, stratagem; (v.), 'shift my bush', i.e. fly to another tree (so that he would have to follow her if he intended to keep her as his target)

SHIPPING, 'good shipping', fine sailing (proverbial phrase for wishing someone good luck)

SHORTNESS, brevity

SHOULD, *see* KNOCK, I ii 13; 'Should ask', Came to ask, III ii 155; 'should die', would have died, III ii 237

SHOULDER-SHOTTEN, with a dislocated shoulder

SHOW, play, pageant, I i 47; i.e. reveal his method, IV i 195; 'show you', show you to be

SHREW, shrewish, IV i 74

SHREWD, ill-natured, shrewish; *see* ILL-FAVOUR'D, I ii 58

SHROW, shrew

SIBYL, a prophetess of Cumae (to whom Apollo gave as many years of life as she could hold grains of sand in her hand)

SIGHT, 'Whose sudden sight', The sudden sight of whom

SIMPLE, foolish, *Induction* i 133, V ii 161

SING IT, sing (i.e. cry out in pain)

SIR LUCENTIO, ('Sir' was a common means of addressing gentlemen who were considered to be foreigners)

SIRRAH, (form of addressing social inferiors)

SITH, since

SKILLS, matters

SKIPPER, flighty fellow

SLACK, remiss, backward

SLASH, *see* SLEEVE

SLEEVE, (perhaps of the 'leg-of-mutton' variety that became popular around 1580. Such sleeves were often slit, padded, and embroidered), IV iii 88

SLENDER, insufficient, IV iv 61

SLIDE, 'let the . . . slide', i.e. let the world go by, don't worry

SLIP, i.e. let the world slide (*see* SLIDE)
SLIPP'D, unleashed
SLIT, (the slitting of someone's nose was a recognised form of revenge)
SMALL, 'small ale', the weakest (and therefore the cheapest) form of ale; 'small choice . . . apples', i.e. little difference between two such horrible things
SMALLEST, weakest (and, hence, cheapest)
SO, If it so, *Induction* i 80; *see* NOUGHT, I i 156; provided that, II i 223, IV iii 16; i.e. what you have just told me, IV ii 88; thus (i.e. according to what he has said), IV iii 192; *see* NONE, V ii 144; 'so money comes withal', provided money comes with it; 'So said, so done, is well', If what he actually does lives up to what he promises, it will be good
SOCRATES' XANTHIPPE, (allusion to Xanthippe, the notoriously shrewish wife of the Greek philosopher Socrates (*c.* 470–399 BC))
SOFT, wait, not so fast, IV iv 23
SOFTLY, gently, I ii 235
SOLEMN, ceremonious
SOL-FA, sing (run up and down musical scales)
SOMETHING, somewhat, a little; (*see* HARD), II i 182
SOOTH, truth; 'Good sooth', Yes indeed; 'sooth to say', to tell the truth
SOPS, dregs, (or 'pieces of cake placed in the cup and soaked in the wine')
SORT, 'in briefer sort', in a quicker fashion
SORTED, 'is sorted . . . proof', has been in vain, to no purpose
SOTO, (perhaps an allusion to a character in John Fletcher's play *Women Pleased*, although, as that play was probably written between 1619 and 1623 (i.e. about thirty years after the probable date at which *The Taming of the Shrew* was written), some commentators believe that it is more probably a reference to an earlier play which was later revised by Fletcher to take the form of *Women Pleased*)
SOUD, (perhaps an expression of impatience; some editors emend the word to read 'Food')
SOUND, 'sound the depth of', get to the bottom of (to 'sound' = to test the depth of water by means of a plumb-line)
SOUNDED, (i) proclaimed, (ii) plumbed (pun)
SPANGLE, brightly adorn
SPAVINS, swellings on the upper hind leg
SPEAK, 'speak of', speak during, *Induction* ii 80

SPECIALITIES, explicitly detailed contracts
SPED, done for, V ii 185; 'sped with', ruined by
SPEED (n.), fortune, successful outcome, II i 137; (v.), *see* HOPE, I ii 243; 'speed amiss', be unsuccessful; 'how speed you', what success are you having
SPEEDING, success
SPIT, 'Spit in the hole', i.e. Moisten the hole into which the peg (on which one end of the treble string is wound) fits so as to tighten the peg and make the string stay in tune longer (probably scornful)
SPITES, vexes
SPLEEN, impulse, mood (the spleen was thought to be the seat of any sudden passion, e.g. of laughter), *Induction* i 135; sudden impulses, whims, III ii 10
SPOIL'D, ruined
SPOKE, spoken
SPORTFUL, amorous
SPRUCE, lively
STAGGERS, a disease which causes a horse to stagger in its gait
STALE, (i) laughingstock, (ii) harlot (pun), I i 58; decoy, lure, III i 88
STAMP, *see* BIG
STAND, withstand, I ii 109; remain, IV iii 44; be (a), IV iv 21; *see* AFFIED, IV iv 50
STANDS, is sufficient (with bawdy pun, *Induction* ii 123), *Induction* ii 122
STARE, glare in anger
STARK SPOIL'D WITH, absolutely ruined by
STARS, 'favourable stars', (allusion to the belief that the configuration of the heavenly bodies could influence the course of the lives of men on earth)
STATE, fortune, I ii 89; rank and degree, V i 111
STAY, restrain, *Induction* i 132; wait, I i 46, III ii 213, V i 85; delay, IV iv 30; 'yet not stay', yet (I) am not content to stay
STAY'D, restrained, held back
STAYS, 'Whatever fortune stays . . . word', i.e. Whatever chance event is at present hindering him from fulfilling your promise; 'stays thy leisure', awaits your permission
STEAD (n.), place, I i 197; (v.), help, I ii 262
STEAL, 'steal our marriage', elope, marry secretly
STEPHEN SLY, (a real Stephen Sly is recorded as living in Stratford-on-Avon in January 1615)
STEPS, i.e. actions, movements

STILL, always, IV i 191, IV iii 189

STOCK, stocking

STOCKS, blocks of wood, i.e. devoid of feelings, I i 31; 'a pair of stocks', i.e. 'I'll have you in the stocks'

STOICS, i.e. people who despise pleasure ('Stoicism' was an austere school of philosophy founded by the Greek Zeno of Citium (c. 362–c. 264 BC) which found great favour with the Romans and which advocated the cultivation of freedom from passions and desires and detachment from the outside world)

STOMACH, appetite, inclination (pun on 'Fall to' = (i) begin, (ii) partake of (food)), I i 38; inclination (to try), I ii 191; (i) appetite, (ii) temper, IV i 142

STOOP, fly to the 'lure' (a bundle of feathers attached to a cord and held by the falconer as a means of recalling a falcon back to him)

STRAIGHT, immediately; immediately go, IV iii 180

STRAND, shore (it seems that Lucentio visualises Jupiter wooing Europa on the island of Crete, and not on Tyre as is the case in Ovid. See DAUGHTER OF AGENOR)

STRANGE, i.e. unnatural a father, I i 85; i.e. surprising, not to be expected, I ii 190

STRANGER, see WALK, II i 83; foreigner, II i 88

STREW'D, see RUSHES

STRUCK, i.e. advanced

STUDIED, 'As she had studied', As if she had bestowed careful study on how

STUDY, learn, II i 255

STUFF, see MASQUING STUFF, IV iii 87; cloth, material, IV iii 118

SUBSCRIBE, submit myself

SUDDEN, see SIGHT, I i 215

SUFFER, 'suffer me', permit me (i.e. to have my own way), II i 31

SUFFICETH, all I need say is, I i 242; it is enough that, III ii 102

SUFFICIENT, 'some sufficient', i.e. the number required by law (to make the contract valid)

SUITS, see IN

SUP, feed, give a supper to

SUPPLY, i.e. fill, III ii 243; i.e. take, fill, III ii 245

SUPPOSES, suppositions, conjectures (allusion to Gascoigne's play Supposes, based on Ariosto's I Suppositi, from which Shakespeare took the Lucentio–Bianca plot)

SWAIN, country bumpkin, II i 203; see PEASANT SWAIN, IV i 113

SWAY, rule, power

SWAY'D . . . BACK, with a wrenched and depressed backbone

SWEAR, 'that one shall swear', so that one is forced to swear

SWEET, scented, sweet-smelling, Induction i 36, Induction i 47

SWEETING, sweetheart

SWIFT, (i) ready-witted, (ii) referring to sweetness (pun), V ii 54

SWINGE ME THEM, beat them

TA'EN, taken; (i) taken, (ii) caught (pun), II i 205; 'ta'en you napping', caught you in the act (i.e. of kissing or courting each other)

TAKE, 'take him for', consider him to be; 'That take it . . . roundly', Who ('That') assume authority so roughly and thoroughly ('roundly') from the very first; 'take upon you', act your part; 'Take up thy mistress' . . . use!', (Grumio pretends to misunderstand and interpret Petruchio's words in a bawdy sense); 'Take no unkindness of', Do not take offence at; 'Take your assurance of her', Make yourself sure of her

TAKES, see TURTLE

TALE, statement, V ii 24

TALES, 'talk of tales', talk idly (pun on 'tail', II i 213)

TALL, clever, able

TALLER, (i) more lofty, (allusion to 'little pot', IV i 4–5), (ii) sturdier, better (pun)

TAMES, 'winter tames . . . beast', (an allusion to the proverb 'Winter and wedlock tame both man and beast')

TAMING-SCHOOL, 'Faith, he is gone unto the taming-school', (It is unclear how Tranio can know this as Hortensio has only just made his decision and has not mentioned his intention to visit Petruchio; this may be evidence to suggest that the play has been imperfectly revised at some stage in its history)

TARRY, wait, delay, Induction ii 123f.

TEMPERATE, cool in mind and temper

TENDER WELL, take good care of

TENTS, bed-hangings

TH'ART, thou art, you are

THAT, what, I ii 82, IV ii 8, IV iv 92; who, II i 88, III ii 231, IV i 68; see TAKE, III ii 210; so that, IV i 167; 'That seeming . . . least are', i.e. That we behave as if we were in the highest degree that which in fact we are not in the least

THEM, i.e. the books, I ii 142, I ii 148; i.e. the words you have just quoted, III i 30; themselves, IV i 4

THESE, those, IV i 179

THEREBY, 'thereby . . . tale', there is a story attached to that

THICK, opaque, V ii 143

THINK, expect, III ii 181; intend, IV iii 188; 'As thou shalt think . . . liv'st!', That you will remember (or 'think twice about') your stupid prattle all your life; 'think for', imagine, IV iii 157

THIRDBOROUGH, constable

THIS, this time, IV v 62

THOU'DST, thou wouldst, you would

THRALL'D, enslaved

THREE-INCH, (i) allusion to Grumio's short stature, (ii) (a phallic jest)

THROUGH, throughout, I i 12

THROUGHLY, thoroughly

THUS, i.e. I shall do so as follows, IV iv 80

THYSELF, you yourself must, I i 240

TIED, obliged, I i 207

TIGHT, watertight, sound

TIME, see IN, II i 194; see FIT, IV iii 69; see MAR, IV iii 97; 'for the time', for the present

'TIS, see MARVEL, IV ii 86; ''Tis a world', It is worth a world, i.e. it is a wonder; ''Tis in my head', I have a plan (and a desire)

TITLE, i.e. 'bride' (perhaps with a pun on 'Title' = legal document of possession; see SEAL), III ii 119

TO, see PROOF, II i 139; i.e. on, II i 147; for, II i 272, II i 356; i.e. let us consider, II i 324; i.e. she will be married to, II i 389; see NOTED, II ii 15; see NOW, III ii 27; compared to, III ii 153; see MAR, IV iii 97; go to, IV iii 180; 'to his liking', see UPON, I ii 179; 'you mean not her to–', i.e. you mean not her to woo; 'to wife', when I marry her, II i 119; 'what to', what about, III ii 40; 'to blame', too blameworthy; 'To her', Attack her, V ii 33f.

TONGUE, 'with my tongue in your tail', i.e. are you going to turn your back on my repartee (with innuendo)

TOOK, struck, III ii 159

TO'T, get on with it, I ii 191

TOUCHETH, concerns, is of importance to

TOWARD, about to begin, I i 68; as a contribution to, II i 97; see CHEER, V i 12; compliant, obedient, V ii 182

TOY, silly trifle, plaything, IV iii 67; 'a toy', sheer nonsense, II i 394

TRAFFIC, business

TRAIN, retinue of attendants

TRAPP'D, adorned with decorated coverings

TREATS OF, deals with

TRENCHERS, wooden dishes

TRANIO, (this is the name of a wily townsman in *Mostellaria*, a play by the Latin playwright Plautus; it may have had connotations arising from its resemblance to 'train' = deceit, trickery)

TRICK, trifle, plaything, IV iii 67

TRICKS, see ELEVEN AND TWENTY, IV ii 57

TRIMM'D UP, luxuriously prepared

TROT, hag, common prostitute

TROW, believe, I ii 4; know, I ii 161

TRUNK SLEEVE, large, wide sleeve

TRUST, 'trust my tale', believe my story; 'never trust me if I be', i.e. I tell you I am not

TRY, test, I ii 18

TUNE, 'when I am in tune', i.e. (i) when I have succeeded in tuning my lute, (ii) when you (Bianca) and I are in harmony

TURN, needs (there may be an unconscious ambiguity: 'turn' can mean 'copulation' in Elizabethan slang), I ii 166; see SERVE, IV ii 62; 'for your turn', suitable for your purpose (with innuendo: 'turn' = copulation), II i 63; exactly suited to you (with innuendo; see above), II i 264

TURN'D, i.e. inside-out (to conceal wear and tear)

TURTLE, turtledove (a symbol of faithful love), II i 206; 'Ay, for a turtle . . . buzzard' (perhaps) the fool will take me for a faithful wife ('turtle', see above) as a turtledove swallows a cockchafer ('buzzard')

TWAIN, two

TWANGLING JACK, twanging knave

'TWAS, It (i.e. 'she') was, II i 320

'TWERE, It would be; would it be, IV i 154; it was, IV iv 12

TWINK, twinkling, instant

TWO, 'two notes', (perhaps a reference to his real and his disguised natures); 'two and thirty . . . out', i.e. (i) aged thirty-two, very nearly, (ii) drunk (slang deriving from the card game 'trentuno' (i.e. 'one-and-thirty'); 'pip' = a spot on a playing card, and 'a pip out' = off by one)

TYRIAN, purple or dark red (originally a reference to the dye anciently made in Tyre from molluscs)

UNABLE WORMS, i.e. poor, weak creatures
UNAPT TO, unfit for
UNCASE, undress
UNDER, see COUNTENANCE, V i 33
UNDERTAKE, agree, promise, I ii 180; adopt, IV ii 106
UNDONE, ruined
UNEXPERIENC'D, uninformed of them
UNHAPPY, harsh, inauspicious
UNKIND, unnaturally hostile
UNPINK'D, 'all unpink'd', entirely lacking in their proper ornamentation (to 'pink' leather = to make a decorated pattern in leather by punching small holes in it)
UNPOLISHED, unrefined, ill-educated, ill-trained
UNPROVIDED, poorly prepared (i.e. dressed)
UNREVERENT, disrespectful
UNTO, 'unto thy master's use', i.e. for the tailor's master to do what he likes with
UNTOWARD, unmannerly
UNWILLING, unwillingly committed
UP, 'up and down', exactly, entirely
UPON, see DO, I ii 107; 'Upon agreement . . . liking', If we meet the terms that he wants (see I ii 211–212); 'upon knowledge', when you know about; 'Upon entreaty have', i.e. Have only to ask and they receive
USE (n.), see UNTO, IV iii 153; i.e. sexual purposes, IV iii 155; (v.) (often =) treat
USUAL PAIN, customary toil
USURP, counterfeit, assume
UT, (corresponds to the modern 'doh', or lowest note, of the musical scale)

VAIL, 'vail your stomachs', lower your pride
VALANCE OF VENICE GOLD, bed-fringes or drapes made of Venetian embroidery in gold thread
VANTAGE, advantage, opportunity
VELURE, velvet
VENT, express
VENTURE, engage in a risky commercial speculation (especially by trading by ship over dangerous seas; (see II i 320–321), II i 319
VERIEST, 'veriest antic', the oddest fellow ('antic' = grotesque, eccentric creature); 'veriest shrew', i.e. most shrewish wife
VERY, complete, I i 122; 'a very', a true, II i 237; 'very name', the mere name (and nothing else), IV iii 32
VIED, i.e. kept giving me in an effort to match my own (to 'vie' = to raise the stakes in a card game)

VILLAIN, base fellow, slave, rogue

WAITS, will be an attendant upon
WALK, 'walk like a stranger', have the bearing of a foreigner (or 'seem to be a foreigner and on your own')
WANING AGE, (allusion to the widespread belief that the fortunes and moral and intellectual qualities of the human race had been in a process of steady decline since Adam and Eve had been excluded from the Garden of Eden)
WANT, lack, be without
WANTON (v.), play amorously, Induction ii 50
WANTS, are lacking, III ii 242; 'wants no', is no lack of
WAR, i.e. blend (perhaps Petruchio imagines 'her' to be blushing), IV v 30
WARM, see KEEP, II i 258
WARRANT, guarantee, assure, I ii 167; 'warrant you', assure you (I will), IV iv 8
WASP, (play on 'buzzard'; see BUZZARD), II i 208
WATCH, look out of, III ii 140; remain awake, IV i 189; stay on watch, keep awake, during, V ii 150; 'watch her', keep her awake (a term from falconry used to denote the technique of establishing mastery over a hawk by depriving it of sleep)
WATCH'D, stayed awake and on watch, IV ii 59
WAY, see MAKE, I i 228
WAYS, roads, IV i 2
WEAR, see REPAIR, IV ii 114
WEARS, is passing
WEEP, see NOW, III ii 27
WEIGHTY, important, IV iv 26
WELCOME, 'your welcome', a welcome for you
WELKIN, sky
WELL, i.e. well-cooked, IV i 153; 'Well seen', very knowledgeable, well versed
WENT, 'Went they not', If they had not gone
WERE, (often =) would be; see POT, IV i 4; 'Were it better', even if I were better; 'You were best', The best thing you could do would be to
WERT, 'wert best', had better
WHAT, see SO, III ii 212; why, IV i 76; 'what countryman', i.e. where do you come from; 'what to', what of, III ii 40
WHEN, (expression of impatience), IV i 127f.
WHERE, 'Where is the life . . . those–', (from an old ballad); 'in place where', in the right

III

place (i.e. where they could fight); 'where away', where are you going

WHEREFORE, why

WHICH, who, IV ii 38; whom, IV v 56

WHILES, 'the whiles', for the present

WHILST, as long as (see THINK), IV iii 113

WHIT, small particle; 'no whit', in no way

WHITE, centre of the target (pun on 'Bianca' = 'white' in Italian), V ii 186

WHITHER AWAY, Where are you going

WHO, see AS, IV iii 13

WHOM, 'whom thou keep'st command', order about your own servants, not me

WHORESON, bastardly, base (a common term of contempt, literally 'son of a whore')

WHOSE, see HAP, I ii 265

WIDOWHOOD, see ASSURE

WIFE, 'to wife', when I marry her, II i 119

WILD, 'wild Kate', (pun on 'wild-cat')

WILL, who will, Induction i 91, IV ii 62; that will, Induction ii 41; will go, II i 306, II i 314, IV iii 165; wish, V ii 100; 'will you', do you want, I i 56; 'Will I live', It is as inevitable as that I shall go on living, i.e. certainly

WILT, desire; 'wilt thou', do you wish to

WINCOT, (a hamlet four miles south of Stratford)

WIND (n.), (i.e. Petruchio implies that excessive lenience has encouraged Katherina's shrewishness), II i 133; (v.), Blow, Induction i 11 Stage Direction

WINDGALLS, soft tumours generally found on the fetlock joint

WINE, (it was customary for the bride and groom to drink a cup of muscadel wine with the wedding-guests)

WISH, recommend, I i 110; commend, I ii 58

WITH, of, III ii 47; by, IV iii 110; see CONSENT, IV iv 35

WITHAL, with; i.e. At the same time, III i 60; see SO, I ii 80; in addition, III ii 25, IV v 49; with it (my explanation), III ii 105

WITLESS, 'witless else her son', otherwise her son would have been an idiot (i.e. for he has no wits of his own)

WITNESS, i.e. express, II i 328; 'with a wit-

ness', i.e. unabashed, outright, with a vengeance

WITNESSES, see GIVE, II i 312

WIVE, 'wive and thrive', (probably an allusion to the proverbs: 'It is hard to wive (i.e. get married) and thrive both in a year', and 'In wiving and thriving a man should take counsel of all the world, lest he light on a curse while he seeks for a blessing); 'wive it', marry

WOMAN'S MAID, 'woman's maid . . . house', i.e. the mistress of the house's maid

WONDER, miracle, II i 401; see MAKE, III ii 187

WONDERFUL, wonderfully, I i 69; i.e. truly surprising, IV ii 15

WOODCOCK, (a bird proverbially easy to trap, hence a synonym for 'dupe, simpleton')

WORD, see STAYS, III ii 23

WORKMANLY, skilfully

WORLD, see 'TIS, II i 303

WOULD, who would, I i 125; I wish that I (see RING), I i 136; wish, I ii 214, V ii 126; I wish that, I i 246; see FAIN, II i 74; 'Would all the world . . . forsworn', I wish that everyone in the world other than Cambio had sworn to have nothing to do with her (i.e. that Bianca should never be able to get a husband; Hortensio never imagines that Bianca would consent to marry such a lowly fellow as a music-master)

WRANGLING, perversely argumentative

WRONG, (i) harm, (ii) disgrace, II i 1; 'The more my wrong', The greater wrong done to me

XANTHIPPE, see SOCRATES' XANTHIPPE

YARD, yardstick, IV iii 112

Y'ARE, You are

YET, up to this moment, Induction i 94; still, even now, Induction ii 65

YOUNG, inexperienced, II i 230; strong, II i 231

YOUNGLING, stripling, novice

YOURSELF, you yourself, II i 282; 'as yourself', as if you yourself, I ii 153